CAN LAB

THE FABIAN SERIES

Series Editor   Ben Pimlott

CAN LABOUR WIN?

Martin Harrop

Andrew Shaw

UNWIN
PAPERBACKS

LONDON SYDNEY WELLINGTON

First published in Great Britain by the Trade Division of Unwin
Hyman Limited, 1989

UNWIN HYMAN LIMITED
15–17 Broadwick Street
London W1V 1FP

Allen & Unwin Australia Pty Ltd
8 Napier Street, North Sydney, NSW 2060, Australia

Allen & Unwin New Zealand Pty Ltd with the Port Nicholson Press
Compusales Building, 75 Ghuznee Street, Wellington, New Zealand

---

British Library Cataloguing in Publication Data

Harrop, Martin
   Can Labour win? – (The Fabian series)
1. Great Britain. Political parties: Labour Party
(Great Britain)
I. Title   II. Shaw, Andrew   III. Series
324.24107
ISBN 0–04–440432–8

Set in 10 on 11 point Garamond by
Latimer Trend & Company Ltd, Plymouth
and printed in Great Britain
by Cox & Wyman Ltd, Reading

Contents

General Editor's Preface

The purpose of the Fabian Research Unit series of short books, written by leading experts, is to help develop a new radicalism based on principles of equality, fairness and social responsibility. The studies are aimed at politicians, civil servants, policy specialists, journalists, party activists and – especially – members of the socially concerned public. They are 'Fabian' in their focus on the political and administrative means of achieving goals. They take no refuge in cautious moderation, but seek instead a rational extremism, exploring the limits of possible progress.

If you are trying to work out a genuinely radical programme, you have difficulties in the face of a right-wing government that is actually carrying through drastic reforms of its own. The biggest difficulty, of course, is the air of unreality that surrounds any proposal until there is the prospect of a transfer of power. At the same time, there is the frustration of trying to shoot at a moving target.

Should you stick doggedly to the substance of old policies, regardless of circumstances? Should you promise to undo most of what has been done during the last ten years? Or should you accept the new measures as a *fait accompli*, however much you may have opposed them when they were introduced? One reason why an affirmative answer to any of these questions is so unpalatable is that it concedes the initiative to the government, and makes the alternative seem either old-fashioned or negative or defeatist.

Yet there is another option. You can observe that the world has indeed moved on and that the problems facing the nation have changed. You can conclude that the action required of a future administration has altered accordingly and that a new programme will have to be more imaginative, not less. You can frankly acknowledge, without concession, that if the Right has broken some of the taboos against innovation, that at least is to be welcomed. And you can look at every issue with a fresh mind, in the search for a serious originality.

Unfortunately, it is easier to call for new ideas than to have them. There exists no philosopher's stone, awaiting its alchemist; advance is more likely to come through hard work than sudden inspiration. Nevertheless there is already a ferment of discussion on policy, as this series shows.

Each book is a personal contribution and does not necessarily reflect the view of the Unit, or of the Fabian Society with which it is associated. Every topic is approached in a different way. Some authors, for example, are more definite in their prescriptions than others. What they have in common is a concern for the future and an impatience with stale arguments inherited from the past. They share a belief that the vogue for reactionary and neo-liberal panaceas cannot be met either by reviving old remedies or by meekly travelling some distance down the Thatcherite road. They also share a belief that it is pointless to offer a solution without analysing the problem first.

What they intend to do is to expose the failure of existing and former policy, including – where appropriate – policy under earlier administrations; to undermine the convenient theory that a requirement of economic efficiency is inequality and social neglect; and, above all, to consider how, in the world as it has become, real needs can be met.

Can Labour Win? is a particularly timely, important and uncomfortable contribution to the series. It differs from other volumes in its focus on the whole range of policy, offering a clinical study of the implications of opinion poll and electoral data for Labour's future. The authors' conclusion, that 'it will require a major transformation of the political landscape for labour to win a majority in 1991', needs to be taken seriously. The book should act as a corrective to those who, in response to Labour's recent recovery, have swung from extreme gloom to excessive optimism.

At the very least, this book's sober analysis points to a continuing need for the party to overhaul its policies and revitalise its image, including but going beyond the proposals of the 1989 review.

Ben Pimlott

Preface

'Can Labour win the next election?' is a question without a definite answer. By this we mean not only that election results are uncertain but also that Labour's position is particularly ambiguous. In this sense Labour differs from the other parties. For surely the Conservatives have a good chance of winning a majority and the centre parties have none. In this book we examine the complexities of Labour's position. Chapter 1 looks at how votes translate into seats in order to show the kinds of result Labour needs for a parliamentary breakthrough at the next election. It also examines the seats Labour needs to gain. Chapter 2 assesses three factors relating to the share of the vote Labour might achieve: the party's underlying support, the number of votes 'up for grabs' and the characteristics of the target voters. The following chapters examine how Labour might increase its support through improvements in its overall image, particularly on competence (Chapter 3) and through its choice of policies (Chapter 4). The conclusion discusses a way forward for Labour and the appendix is a background briefing about changes in the society Labour seeks to govern and their electoral implications.

Our main purpose is to present a wide range of evidence for readers to consider. Clearly this reflects our judgement of what is reliable information and we have made extensive use of sample surveys, opinion polls and social statistics. This evidence is a good way of identifying strengths on which Labour can build and weaknesses which still need to be worked on. However, we do not suggest that the policy programme should be developed solely or even mainly on the basis of opinion polls. Labour must seek to lead public opinion as well as respond.

Despite the quantity of data now available, interpretation is still as much an art as a science. Our judgements are fallible and the responsibility for any errors of fact or interpretation rests with us and not the originators of the data.

One point about style. For brevity and readability we have not included full technical details of all our methods and sources (though the main sources are listed at the end of the book). Readers who would like more details about any particular finding are asked to contact us directly.

We have worked together on each chapter and have generally reached shared conclusions. None the less, we do not agree on every single point. For the record, then, Andrew Shaw was primarily responsible for Chapters 1, 2 and 5; Martin Harrop for Chapters 3 and 4.

We thank all those involved in producing the information on which this book is based – both the staff of research organisations and their multitude of respondents. We are grateful to John Curtice and Michael Steed for making available constituency election results; to Robert Wybrow for permission to quote the findings of Gallup polls; to the organisers of the British Election Studies, the British Social Attitude surveys and the BBC/Gallup surveys for making their data available for further analysis; and to the ESRC Data Archive for supplying much of the data. Our analysis of the Election Studies used the educational data-sets developed by John Curtice and Andrew Shaw. For specific help and advice we thank Hugh Berrington, Ivor Crewe, John Curtice, Stan Openshaw and Ben Pimlott. We are grateful for permission from copyright-holders to reproduce cartoons and advertisements. Finally, our thanks to family and friends for their support during the writing of this book.

By July 1989, Labour's image had improved enough to ensure the government could no longer ride out economic difficulties. But on underlying indicators such as ratings for competence, unity and leadership, Labour stayed behind the Conservatives. Assuming a swing back to the government before the election, our judgement remains that while Labour can dream of victory, it should plan for a hung Parliament.

Martin Harrop
Andrew Shaw
July 1989

Part I

The Task

Chapter 1
Seats

This chapter examines the electoral arithmetic of Labour's task in 1991 or 1992 (hereafter we use '1991' as shorthand for 1991/2). We look first at the relationship between votes and seats. What outcomes in votes will (a) deny the Conservatives an overall majority of seats and (b) give Labour a majority? (a) The Conservatives will lose their majority if they finish with less than 39 per cent of the vote. (To win a majority with 39 per cent or more, the Conservatives need a lead over Labour in the range of two to four points.) (b) For Labour to win a majority a lead over the Conservatives of four or five points will be needed.

Secondly, we examine the marginals which Labour needs to win: do they have any common characteristics which should be reflected in Labour's strategy? The simple answer is 'no'. The target seats cover a broad range, though most of the southern marginals are urban seats.

Seats and Votes

Table 1.1 sets out seat projections for various shares of the vote at the next election, assuming 'uniform swing'. This means that whatever the change in each party's share of the vote in 1991, we assume this will be the same in every constituency in Great Britain. Of course, reality will be more complicated; there are sure to be some exceptional results and, in all probability, a continuation of regional trends in voting. This makes uniform swing unsatisfactory for predicting which specific seats will change hands, but does not make the overall projection unreliable. For example, in 1987 the Conservatives won seventeen seats which they would not have done under uniform swing but this was just about balanced by fifteen unanticipated losses, so producing an accurate overall prediction. The uniform swing method fared less well with Labour. Its gains were overestimated by eight, due mainly to an 'incumbency effect' which enabled a number of Conservative MPs who won seats from Labour in 1983 to hold on in 1987 (Curtice and Steed, in Butler and Kavanagh, 1988). There were only five such gains in 1987, so this will be far less important in 1991. Therefore, unless there is extraordinary political change, the overall projection should be reliable. If there is a major political earthquake, the projections should be treated cautiously.

Table 1.1 is calculated on the basis of one SLD or SDP candidate in each constituency and an unchanged nationalist vote.

The table of projections puts the position of each of the parties in perspective.

For Labour, it shows how difficult it will be to win a majority at the next election. Labour has to win *at least* 39 per cent of the votes *and* lead the Conservatives by at least four percentage points for this to happen. Labour has achieved this only once in the last twelve elections – in 1966, when it was already in office. Put another way, Labour needs over twice as big a swing from the Conservatives as it has recorded at any election since 1945. Any hope taken from the fact that Labour won in 1964 after three Conservative victories in the 1950s is false comfort. Labour finished only four points behind in 1959. A repeat in 1991 of the 1964 swing to Labour would still leave the Conservatives with a six point lead!

As well as showing the scale of Labour's task, Table 1.1 also reveals a dilemma for Labour with regard to the centre party(ies). For while Labour does not want the Democrats to do well, neither should it want them to do very badly. Labour is unlikely to take many votes directly from the Conservatives. Switching between the two biggest parties is uncommon. Conservative voters are more likely to change to another opposition party (or possibly to deliberate abstention). This still helps Labour, given that Labour needs the Conservative vote to fall. So it is completely wrong to say that the votes of disaffected Conservatives for opposition parties other than Labour cannot help to defeat Thatcher. Furthermore, while Labour could gain from a squeeze on the third party in marginal seats, it is less likely to benefit from a general collapse of the centre parties' vote. Recall that when the Alliance disintegrated after the last election the Conservatives' poll ratings were in the high forties or even more. Also, in the 1983 to 1987 Parliament, the only poll figures which would have produced a Labour majority occurred when the Alliance scored in the mid to high twenties (or even the low thirties). Labour never had a winning lead when the Alliance was below twenty-three. And in 1988, as the SLD and SDP languished, Labour led in not one month. For the next election, Labour needs to win well in its competition for votes with all other parties, but hope the centre parties are credible enough to gain a good share of the votes for which they compete with the Conservatives.

For the Conservatives Table 1.1 reveals a position of undoubted strength. Even if Labour cuts the 1987 gap of twelve points to just four points, the Conservatives should stay in power. What is more, with uniform swing, a 43:40 result may well give the Conservatives a majority, while the reverse would leave Labour a handful of seats short. And in the event of a tie at 40 per cent, the Conservatives may well get more seats and perhaps even enough to govern with the support of only the Ulster Unionists. However, this advantage to the Conservatives from the electoral system does depend on their votes continuing to be more efficiently spread between safe and marginal seats.

The strength of the Conservative position should not be overstated, though. A loss of votes on the scale of 1964 or February 1974 would cost them outright power, if not necessarily their status as largest party in the Commons.

For the Democrats and the SDP, Table 1.1 reveals the continuing inequity of the electoral system. Even if they were to achieve 28 per cent of the vote, they would win only 5–10 per cent of the seats – and this is assuming only one centre party candidate per seat! However, if the centre parties' share of the vote is very low, they will almost certainly retain more seats than is shown in some projections. Consider the seats currently held by these parties listed in order of majority in Table 1.2. The Democrats have eight seats which appear safe, notwithstanding the more pessimistic projections in Table 1.1. These are all those with greater than 10 per cent majorities, except Inverness, Nairn & Lochaber, where the 1987 win was based on a little more than a third of the vote. In addition, the Democrats may retain more

LABOUR SHARE OF THE VOTE

%	25	26	27	28	29	30	31	32	33
33									
34			*Note:* C=Conservative seats; L=Labour seats; D=SLD and SDP seats. The relevant SLD plus SDP share is found by subtracting the sum of the Conservative and Labour shares from *98* (leaving 2 per cent for the nationalists and others). Not shown are projected wins by nationalists (between 5 and 7) and seats in Northern Ireland (17). There are 650 seats in the Commons. In 1987, the Conservatives won 376 seats, Labour 229, Liberals 17, Nationalists 6 and the SDP 5.						
35									
36									
37									C 31 / L 26 / D 4
38								C 322 / L 258 / D 47	C 32 / L 26 / D 4
39							C 340 / L 245 / D 42	C 338 / L 249 / D 40	C 33 / L 26 / D 3
40						C 351 / L 235 / D 41	C 352 / L 241 / D 34	C 348 / L 245 / D 34	C 34 / L 25 / D 3
41					C 367 / L 224 / D 35	C 361 / L 232 / D 34	C 357 / L 236 / D 34	C 353 / L 243 / D 31	C 35 / L 24 / D 2
42				C 375 / L 215 / D 36	C 371 / L 220 / D 35	C 368 / L 226 / D 33	C 364 / L 232 / D 31	C 365 / L 238 / D 24	C 36 / L 24 / D 2
43			C 390 / L 200 / D 36	C 385 / L 207 / D 34	C 378 / L 217 / D 31	C 379 / L 222 / D 26	C 376 / L 228 / D 23	C 371 / L 234 / D 22	C 368 / L 23 / D 21
44		C 399 / L 189 / D 38	C 396 / L 197 / D 33	C 398 / L 201 / D 27	C 393 / L 208 / D 25	C 385 / L 218 / D 24	C 382 / L 224 / D 21	C 378 / L 228 / D 21	C 372 / L 234 / D 21
45	C 408 / L 182 / D 36	C 411 / L 187 / D 28	C 407 / L 193 / D 26	C 403 / L 199 / D 24	C 401 / L 202 / D 23	C 395 / L 211 / D 21	C 386 / L 220 / D 21	C 385 / L 224 / D 18	C 381 / L 228 / D 18
46	C 418 / L 178 / D 30	C 415 / L 185 / D 26	C 414 / L 188 / D 24	C 409 / L 194 / D 23	C 404 / L 199 / D 23	C 404 / L 205 / D 18	C 398 / L 211 / D 18	C 389 / L 220 / D 18	C 385 / L 227 / D 15
47	C 426 / L 176 / D 25	C 421 / L 182 / D 24	C 417 / L 187 / D 23	C 418 / L 189 / D 20	C 413 / L 196 / D 18	C 408 / L 202 / D 18	C 405 / L 205 / D 18	C 399 / L 211 / D 18	C 392 / L 224 / D 12
48	C 429 / L 173 / D 25	C 429 / L 177 / D 21	C 424 / L 183 / D 20	C 420 / L 187 / D 20	C 418 / L 191 / D 18	C 413 / L 197 / D 18	C 410 / L 202 / D 16	C 408 / L 208 / D 12	C 403 / L 215 / D 10

(Left axis, top to bottom: **CONSERVATIVE SHARE OF THE VOTE**)

CONSERVATIVE MAJORITY

Vote in Great Britain

LABOUR SHARE OF THE VOTE

34	35	36	37	38	39	40	41	42	43	
			C 251 L 313 D 62	C 247 L 323 D 56	C 248 L 328 D 50	C 246 L 338 D 42	C 248 L 342 D 36	C 242 L 352 D 32	C 242 L 356 D 28	**LABOUR MAJORITY**
		C 266 L 301 D 59	C 266 L 306 D 54	C 261 L 316 D 49	C 259 L 328 D 39	C 256 L 335 D 35	C 255 L 342 D 29	C 255 L 345 D 26	C 250 L 354 D 22	
	C 283 L 290 D 54	C 280 L 296 D 51	C 280 L 303 D 44	C 276 L 310 D 41	C 273 L 322 D 32	C 267 L 331 D 29	C 265 L 338 D 24	C 261 L 343 D 23	C 259 L 347 D 21	
295 279 53	C 294 L 287 D 46	C 293 L 290 D 44	C 291 L 298 D 38	C 288 L 308 D 31	C 287 L 315 D 25	C 280 L 323 D 24	C 271 L 333 D 23	C 266 L 340 D 21	C 264 L 345 D 18	
306 277 44	C 307 L 281 D 39	C 303 L 288 D 36	C 304 L 293 D 30	C 298 L 304 D 25	C 293 L 310 D 24	C 288 L 316 D 23	C 283 L 324 D 20	C 277 L 335 D 15	C 271 L 341 D 15	
319 271 37	C 318 L 277 D 32	C 314 L 282 D 31	C 308 L 293 D 26	C 305 L 298 D 24	C 301 L 305 D 21	C 300 L 311 D 16	C 294 L 317 D 16	C 287 L 326 D 14	C 278 L 335 D 14	
329 266 32	C 324 L 272 D 31	C 319 L 279 D 29	C 317 L 288 D 22	C 315 L 295 D 17	C 311 L 299 D 17	C 306 L 306 D 15	C 301 L 312 D 14	C 295 L 318 D 14	C 287 L 327 D 13	
335 261 31	C 332 L 267 D 28	C 331 L 277 D 19	C 325 L 284 D 18	C 322 L 289 D 16	C 316 L 296 D 15	C 312 L 300 D 15	C 306 L 307 D 14	C 304 L 312 D 11	C 298 L 319 D 10	**HUNG PARLIAMENT**
352 252 23	C 342 L 262 D 23	C 338 L 272 D 17	C 332 L 279 D 16	C 326 L 285 D 16	C 322 L 290 D 15	C 319 L 297 D 11	C 315 L 301 D 11	C 309 L 308 D 10	C 304 L 313 D 10	
357 248 22	C 354 L 255 D 18	C 343 L 267 D 17	C 338 L 273 D 16	C 335 L 280 D 12	C 329 L 286 D 12	C 325 L 291 D 11	C 319 L 297 D 11	C 315 L 302 D 10	C 311 L 308 D 8	
363 243 21	C 358 L 252 D 17	C 357 L 257 D 13	C 346 L 268 D 13	C 341 L 274 D 12	C 335 L 281 D 11	C 329 L 287 D 11	C 327 L 292 D 8	C 321 L 298 D 8	C 318 L 302 D 7	
371 241 15	C 366 L 247 D 14	C 361 L 253 D 13	C 357 L 258 D 12	C 346 L 269 D 12	C 343 L 275 D 9	C 338 L 281 D 8	C 332 L 288 D 7	C 328 L 292 D 7	C 323 L 299 D 5	
375 238 14	C 371 L 243 D 13	C 366 L 248 D 13	C 363 L 254 D 10	C 360 L 259 D 8	C 350 L 270 D 7	C 345 L 275 D 7	C 340 L 281 D 6	C 333 L 288 D 6	C 329 L 293 D 5	
381 232 14	C 377 L 239 D 11	C 374 L 244 D 9	C 370 L 249 D 8	C 365 L 255 D 7	C 362 L 259 D 6	C 351 L 270 D 6	C 346 L 275 D 6	C 340 L 282 D 5		
389 229 10	C 386 L 233 D 9	C 380 L 240 D 8	C 377 L 245 D 6	C 372 L 250 D 6	C 367 L 255 D 6	C 363 L 259 D 6	C 352 L 270 D 6			
394 225 9	C 391 L 230 D 7	C 388 L 234 D 6	C 382 L 240 D 6	C 377 L 245 D 6	C 372 L 250 D 6	C 368 L 255 D 5				

CONSERVATIVE MAJORITY

DAILY Mirror STOP

Thursday, June 9, 1983   16p

THE WASTE OF OUR NATION

..for your job your children and your future

Vote Labour

Thursday, June 9, 1983

Labour's lone voice in the daily press, plugging away in 1983.

Table 1.2 SLD and SDP Seats

(SLD *unless SDP shown*)	Majority in 1987 (%)	2nd party	Con (%)	Lab (%)	Lib/ SDP (%)	Nation- alist (%)
Caithness & Sutherland	36.9	Con	16.7	14.9	53.6*	10.3
Ross, Cromarty & Skye	29.7	Con	19.7	19.1	49.4*	11.8
Berwick-upon-Tweed	22.6	Con	29.5	17.5	52.1	
Tweeddale, Ettrick & Lauderdale	20.3	Con	29.6	11.4	49.9	9.1
Orkney & Shetland	18.4	Con	23.3	18.7	41.7	14.5†
Gordon	17.6	Con	31.9	11.5	49.5	7.2
Plymouth Devonport (SDP)	13.0	Con	29.3	28.5	42.3*	
Roxburgh & Berwickshire	12.0	Con	37.2	8.8	49.2	4.8
Inverness, Nairn & Lochaber	11.5	Lab	23.0	25.3	36.8	14.8
Yeovil	10.2	Con	41.3	7.3	51.4	
Ceredigion & Pembroke North	9.7	Con	26.9	18.6	36.6	16.2
Truro	8.2	Con	40.8	10.2	49.0	
Montgomery	8.1	Con	38.5	10.5	46.6	4.5
Southwark & Bermondsey	7.7	Lab	12.6	39.7	47.4	
Greenwich (SDP)	5.7	Lab	23.3	34.9	40.6*	
Rochdale	5.4	Lab	18.6	38.0	43.4	
Liverpool, Mossley Hill	4.9	Lab	17.5	38.8	43.7	
Woolwich (SDP)	4.7	Lab	21.2	37.0	41.7*	
Argyll & Bute	3.8	Con	33.5	12.1	37.3	17.1
Fife North East	3.6	Con	41.2	7.4	44.8	6.6
Southport	3.4	Con	44.5	6.4	47.9	
Brecon & Radnor	0.1	Con	34.7	29.2	34.8	1.3

* = SDP 1987

† = Orkney & Shetland Movement

seats than predicted through the personal votes of sitting MPs. This applies particularly to the three seats first won by the Alliance in 1987 – Fife North East, Argyll & Bute, and Southport. In a tight race this could deny the Conservatives a projected overall majority. For example, the projected result for an outcome of Conservative – 43; Labour – 41; Democrats – 14 gives the Conservatives a tiny majority. But would the Conservatives actually pick up projected wins in the Democrat seats of Argyll & Bute, Fife North East, Montgomery, Southport and Truro? The precise number of Labour seats may also depend on whether it actually makes expected gains from the SLD and SDP. But Labour is second in only six SLD/SDP seats and should gain most of these before it comes close to winning a majority. So there is very little chance that outcomes in centre– Labour marginals will critically affect the balance of power in the Commons.

For all parties, Table 1.1 reveals the need for contingency planning against a hung Parliament. Though Labour finished twelve points behind in 1987, against only four points in 1959, there is now a far wider range of results which will produce a hung Parliament. Compare the substantial leads needed now with the projection after 1959 that Labour needed only a 2 per cent lead, and the Conservatives merely parity in the popular vote, to secure a majority! This change is partly due to the improved fortunes of other parties. After 1959, there were just six Liberals and a solitary independent; after 1987, there were forty-five MPs from other parties, including the seventeen from Northern Ireland. But there has also been a substantial decline in the number of Conservative–Labour marginals. A given lead in votes is now translated into a far smaller lead in seats. There is still enough bias in the system to produce majorities when one party obtains a reasonable lead in votes. But we will surely have a hung Parliament before too long.

By assuming the minor parties will win just 2 per cent, the table makes no allowance for the rise of the Greens. Any realistic increase in the Green vote is unlikely to make the projections unreliable, except where Democrat gains are shown (unlikely!). The Greens will have more impact on the vote for other parties than on how votes are translated into seats.

How might continuing regional changes (Table 1.3) affect the distribution of seats in 1991? The answer appears to be not very

Table 1.3 Regional Changes in Vote Shares, 1983–7 – Constituency Averages

	North/West Britain	*South/East Britain (excluding Devon and Cornwall)*	*Devon and Cornwall*
Conservative	−2.7	+1.2	−3.1
Labour	+6.5	+1.6	+2.6
Alliance	−4.2	−2.5	+0.7

Note: 'North/West Britain' includes Scotland, Wales and the North of England; the 'South/East' is, therefore, the Midlands, East Anglia and South of England. The boundary lies between the counties of Cheshire, Greater Manchester, West Yorkshire, South Yorkshire and Humberside, which are in the North/West, and Staffordshire, Derbyshire, Nottinghamshire and Lincolnshire, which are in the South/East.

Source: Curtice and Steed, in Butler and Kavanagh (1988).

much. On one method of allowing for intensification of the North–South divide, Labour could actually gain more seats in 1991 than it did in 1987 should the 1983 to 1987 changes be repeated. But another method gives Labour around the same number of seats as a uniform swing projection (see box on p. 12 for details).

Of course, a repeat of 1983 to 1987 changes will leave the Conservatives with a majority in 1991. We therefore extended this analysis to a range of vote shares which might produce a hung Parliament or a Labour majority. This means making more questionable assumptions, so the conclusions are tentative. But we found that an intensification of divisions between South/East and North/West Britain should not make it harder to wipe out the Conservative majority. In seeking to achieve this, Labour can afford to do even better in the North/West than in the South/East but not, of course, to improve only in the North/West.

However, growing regional variations could make it even more difficult for Labour to win an outright majority. Only 43 per cent of the seats in Britain are in the North/West. Labour has not yet reached the point of diminishing returns in this area. But this could well happen if Labour were to get near to a parliamentary majority. Though this is not a likely prospect in 1991, there could be a problem for Labour in subsequent elections, especially as the proportion of the population living in North/West Britain is declining (Table 1.4).

Analysing the Impact of Intensification of the North–South Divide – Technical Details

The table below projects the result of the next election in three separate situations:

A. *Uniform swing*   This assumes the 1991 election is a rerun in every constituency of the national change between 1983 and 1987: Conservative -0.2; Labour $+3.2$; SLD -3.0. This is a baseline projection which assumes no intensification of the regional divisions in 1991.

B. *Regional change*   This assumes that vote shares in every constituency change next time in accordance with the average regional change in 1987 (see Table 1.3). This allows at a broad level for the same intensification of regional divisions as occurred in 1987.

C. *Individual constituency change*   This assumes that vote shares in every constituency change next time as they did between 1983 and 1987. This is an alternative way of allowing for continued growth in the regional divide. It does, though, overestimate the number of SLD/SDP seats because it is unrealistically assumed that some excellent constituency results by the Alliance in 1987 will be repeated. Allowing for this, Labour is not shown to be worse off in seats.

	Number of seats		
	Conservative	*Labour*	*SLD/SDP*
A. Uniform swing	360	250	17
B. Regional change	352	256	19
C. Individual constituency change	352	247	28

This should favour the Conservatives, as might other population shifts; for example, to more affluent areas within the non-metropolitan South. As a result of these movements the electorates in many Conservative seats are already very large but in

Table 1.4 Population 1986 and 2001 Projection (millions)

	1986	*2001*
North/West Britain		
Scotland	5.1	5.1
Wales	2.8	2.9
North	3.1	3.0
North-West	6.4	6.3
Yorkshire & Humberside	4.9	4.9
	22.3	22.2
	(40.4%)	(38.7%)
South/East Britain		
West Midlands	5.2	5.3
East Midlands	3.9	4.2
East Anglia	2.0	2.3
South-East	10.5	11.5
Greater London	6.8	6.9
South-West	4.5	5.0
	32.9	35.2
	(59.6%)	(61.3%)

Source: OPCS Population Projections: Area (London: HMSO, 1988).

many Labour seats are particularly small. Indeed, the Conservatives represent ninety-five of the seats with the 100 largest electorates (1988 figures) in England. This implies that the next boundary revision, not due to begin until 1991, will cost Labour seats (even allowing for continued over-representation of Scotland and Wales at Westminster). Precisely how many depends on the exact nature of the population shifts and the extent to which the North–South and urban–rural divides in voting sharpen further. However, Curtice and Steed estimate in Butler and Kavanagh (1988) that Labour could lose eleven seats from the next redistribution and Jeff Rooker's conclusion is similar – a minimum net loss of about ten seats.

The Decisive Marginals

The central task at the next election, in our view, is to deprive the Conservatives of a majority. This means ensuring that over fifty fewer Conservatives are elected than in 1987. Labour cannot rely on the other opposition parties winning any of these.

Indeed, the Conservatives might pick up a few SLD seats. So exactly how many Conservative seats Labour must win depends on the SLD, SDP, SNP and PC. In any case, there will always be upsets – surprise gains and unexpected failures. In analysing the Conservative-held marginals, we need a list of seats long enough to ensure Labour's success if virtually all are won. To be sure of preventing another Conservative majority, we assume Labour needs to take nearly sixty Conservative seats, and so we present a 'top sixty' list.

There is also a second group we should look at – the additional seats Labour would have to win to gain a majority. Ninety-six seats, plus the recapture of Govan, would see Labour to power, which we adjust upwards to a round 100. This would be cutting it too fine if the prospect became real, but we do mention some other seats in the discussion below.

The 100 seats have been selected on the simple basis of the smallest gaps between Labour and the party holding the seat. In Table 1.5, giving details of these, the eight SLD/SDP seats with the smallest majorities over Labour are included in the appropriate position among the Conservative-held seats.

The list of sixty Con–Lab marginals can be adjusted in anticipation of increased regional variation in voting. If, in North/West Britain, the average change for Labour is 5 per cent greater (and for the Conservatives is 3 per cent lower) than in South/East Britain, then a seat in the North/West with a majority 8 per cent greater than one in the South/East is actually as good a prospect for Labour. On this basis, the following changes would be made to the 'top sixty' list:

In	*Out*
Vale of Glamorgan	Harlow
Bury North	Nuneaton
Chorley	Croydon North West
South Ribble	Luton South
Lancaster	Feltham & Heston
Eastwood	Lewisham West
Edinburgh West	Bristol East

So Labour can afford to fail in, for example, Nuneaton and Luton South, only if it wins in the likes of Bury North and Lancaster.

A further point is that Labour finished third last time in some target seats. Labour can win from third. In 1987, it took four seats – Clwyd South West, Edinburgh South, Renfrew West & Inverclyde, and Strathkelvin & Bearsden – where it had finished just behind the second-placed Alliance in 1983. On this basis, the two seats in the top sixty in which Labour finished third last time, Stockton South and Colne Valley, are perfectly good prospects. But where Labour is a long way behind two parties the job is more difficult since Labour is subject to a 'tactical squeeze' which can hamper the party perceived to lie third. This applies, though, in only one of the above seats, Edinburgh West, which is thus clearly not one of the top sixty targets even if regional trends do continue.

Equivalent points apply to the list of 100 seats which Labour needs for outright victory. Using the same eight point adjustment for regional trends, eleven seats in the South/East are not as good prospects as others in the North/West:

In	*Out*
Davyhulme	Derbyshire South
Conwy	Dudley West
Dumfries	Peterborough
Blackpool North	Norwich North
Littleborough & Saddleworth	Erith & Crayford
Ceredigion & Pembroke North	Eltham
Cardiff North	Gravesham
Monmouth	Edmonton
Leeds North East	Fulham
Leeds North West	Brentford & Isleworth
Wirral South	Putney

Here, in terms of specific seats, is evidence that regional trends could make it even more difficult for Labour to win a majority. To compensate for failing to capture some of the southern seats, Labour would have to make some astonishing gains in the North/West. Indeed, in 1987 Labour finished third in five of

Table 1.5 The 'Top 100' Marginals Labour Needs to Gain for a Majority, with Comments on the 'Top 60' Conservative-held Marginals Labour Needs to Gain to Prevent a Conservative Majority

Constituency	Majority over Labour 1987	Winner 1979 (Notional) 1983	Winner 1987	1987 Result (%) change since 1983 Con	Lab	Alliance (*SDP)	Other(s)	Comment
York	147 0·2%	Lab	Con	Con	41·6 +0·3	41·4 +6·3	15·9* −7·1	1·0 +0·4	Held by Labour 1966–83. A large electorate based on York city. Will Nestlé's takeover of Rowntree help Labour?
Ayr	182 0·3%	Con	Con	Con	39·4 −3·4	39·1 +12·3	14·8 −10·8	6·7 +1·8	George Younger's seat since 1964. A massive swing from the Alliance to Labour in 1987. A mixture of council estates and professional areas.
Wolverhampton North East	204 0·4%	Lab	Lab	Con	42·1 +2·5	41·7 +1·6	16·2 −2·9		Renee Short's seat 1964–87. Incumbency effect may help the Conservatives in 1991.
Dulwich	180 0·5%	Con	Con	Con	42·4 +1·9	42·0 +6·3	14·5* −7·5	1·1	The Conservatives gained Sam Silkin's old seat in 1983, helped by boundary changes. Divided between the 'affluent village' and the seedy hinterland'. The former contains Mrs Thatcher's Barratt home.
Wallasey	279 0·5%	Con	Con	Con	42·5 −3·5	41·9 +9·5	15·6* −6·0		Always winnable, never won, despite a good performance in 1987. Ernest Marples, then Lynda Chalker, have held on. Diverse: docks, estates, commuterland, resort.

Constituency	Majority				Shares & swings				Notes
Nottingham East	456 *1.0%*	Lab	Con	Con	42.9 *+2.5*	42.0 *+4.9*	14.7 *−4.6*	0.5	A socially divided strip along the edge of town though still predominantly working class. A new seat where Sharon Atkin was suspended as Labour candidate before the last election.
Thurrock	690 *1.4%*	Lab	Lab	Con	42.5 *+7.1*	41.0 *+1.9*	16.5* *−5.2*		One of Labour's few prospects in the South outside London. Conservative gain from Oonagh McDonald in 1987 so the incumbency effect may help the Conservatives in 1991.
Ipswich	874 *1.7%*	Lab	Lab	Con	44.4 *+2.8*	42.7 *−1.0*	12.6* *−1.7*	0.3 *−0.2*	A Labour seat for 50 years (except 1970–Oct. 1974) before Ken Weetch's defeat in 1987 with the highest vote share of any Labour loser. Incumbency effect may help the Conservatives in 1991.
Bolton North East	813 *1.7%*	Con	Con	Con	44.4 *+1.2*	42.6 *+4.8*	13.0* *−5.3*		A new seat won by the Conservatives in 1983 and retained with the help of the incumbency effect in 1987. Mixes the depressed Central Ward with salubrious, more rural areas. Contains most of the old 'barometer' seat of Bolton East.
Battersea	857 *1.8%*	Lab	Lab	Con	44.2 *+7.9*	42.4 *−1.4*	11.9* *−5.6*	1.4 *−0.9*	'A moderately safe Labour seat', wrote Waller before the Conservatives' dramatic gain in 1987 with a 7.9% increase in their share of the vote. Gentrification helped. Incumbency effect may help the Conservatives in 1991.

Table 1.5 — contd

Constituency	Majority over Labour 1987	Winner 1979 (National) 1983	Winner 1987	1987 Result (%) change since 1983 Con	Lab	Alliance (*SDP)	Other(s)	Comment
Stirling	948 2·1%	Con	Con	38·3 −1·7	36·2 +8·3	14·8 −9·1	10·7 +2·5	A new, large seat including Stirling University and the Trossachs. The Conservatives won in 1983 on a big swing (for Scotland) which was not completely reversed in 1987.
Lancashire West	1,353 2·2%	Con	Con	43·7 −2·5	41·5 +7·7	14·8* −5·2		Despite a comfortable Conservative victory in 1983, Waller predicted a close contest in 1987 and was right. Labour may have been helped by its strong performance in nearby Liverpool.
Batley and Spen	1,362 2·3%	Lab	Con	43·4 +3·9	41·1 +3·2	14·3* −7·3	1·2	In 1987 the incumbency effect helped the new Conservative MP to retain this new Pennines textiles marginal.
Delyn	1,224 2·3%	Con	Con	41·4 −0·2	39·1 +9·7	17·0 −8·8	2·5 −0·7	Possibly helped by a high turnout, Labour cut the Conservative majority by 4,720 in this seat on the Dee Estuary in NE Wales.
Hornsey and Wood Green	1,779 3·0%	Con	Con	43·0 +0·5	40·0 +4·9	15·1* −5·8	2·0 +0·3	Labour's vote went up by over 5,000 in 1987 in this mixed seat with a large non-white population in Hornsey and an affluent professional section east of Hampstead Heath

Constituency	Electorate								Notes
Ellesmere Port and Neston	1,853 3·2%	Lab	Con	Con	44·4 −1·5	41·2 +8·6	14·1* −7·4	0·3	Labour bounced back in 1987 after a dismal result in 1983. Based on the industrial centre of Ellesmere Port but balanced by Conservative commuters in Neston and the villages.
Langbaurgh	2,088 3·3%	Con	Con	Con	41·7 0·0	38·4 +7·0	19·9 −7·0		Labour needs to continue squeezing the Alliance here. A mixture of rural communities in the Cleveland Hills, resorts and what remains of the heavy industry of South Middlesbrough.
Corby	1,805 3·4%	Lab	Con	Con	44·3 +1·7	40·9 +4·8	14·8 −5·4		The steel works closure caused massive unemployment but the constituency also includes hunting territory in East Northants.
Stockton South	2,233 3·8%	Lab	SDP	Con	35·0 −1·5	31·3 +5·0	33·7* −3·0		A Conservative gain from the SDP in 1987. The Conservative share fell but Ian Wrigglesworth's fell further as Labour moved to a close third. A constituency of home-owners.
Nottingham South	2,234 4·2%	Con	Con	Con	45·0 −0·9	40·8 +6·7	14·1* −5·9		A new, mixed seat, containing large council estates and Conservative areas around the university. Substantial non-white population.
Walthamstow	1,512 4·3%	Lab	Lab	Con	39·0 +3·1	34·7 −5·1	25·1* +3·5	1·1 −1·5	A safe Labour seat in 1979, Eric Deakins lost after a sharp fall in his vote in 1987. Small electorate. High Alliance vote for a Con–Lab marginal. Incumbency effect may help the Conservatives in 1991.

Table 1.5 —contd

Constituency	Majority over Labour 1987	Winner 1979 (Notional) 1983		Winner 1987	1987 Result (%) change since 1983 Con	Lab	Alliance (*SDP)	Other(s)	Comment
Tynemouth	2,583 4·4%	Con	Con	Con	43·2 −5·4	38·8 +7·5	18·0 −2·1		Labour has not won here since 1945 and Neville Trotter has been in place since 1974. The last Conservative seat on Tyneside. Some council estates but principally middle-class residential areas.
Hyndburn	2,220 4·6%	Lab	Con	Con	44·4 +2·1	39·8 −2·4	15·2* +0·6	0·6 −0·4	In 1987 the incumbency effect helped the Conservatives increase their majority by over 2,000 in this classic Lancashire marginal. Skilled workers in owner-occupied terraces in small ex-textile towns.
Woolwich	1,937 4·7%	Lab	SDP	SDP	21·2 −3·9	37·0 +3·6	41·7* +1·2		John Cartwright hung on for the SDP in 1987 but Labour will surely regain this working-class seat next time.
Cardiff Central	1,986 4·8%	Con	Con	Con	37·1 −4·4	32·3 +8·1	29·4 −3·2	1·3 −0·5	A traditional Conservative seat, based on the old Cardiff North. Labour needs to squeeze the strong Alliance vote. High proportion of service sector professionals, little council housing.

Constituency	Majority								Notes
Liverpool, Mossley Hill	2,226 4·9%	Con	Lib	Lib	17·5 −14·3	38·8 +12·0	43·7 +2·8		A massive swing from the Conservatives to Labour in 1987 was not enough to dislodge Liberal David Alton. A new constituency of large social contrasts.
Birmingham, Selly Oak	2,584 4·9%	Con	Con	Con	44·2 −0·7	39·3 +4·9	15·4 −5·3	1·2	A traditional Conservative seat regained by Anthony Beaumont-Dark in 1979 after a Labour flourish in October 1974. A mixed seat with a sprinkling of students and non-whites.
Hampstead and Highgate	2,221 4·9%	Con	Con	Con	42·5 +1·3	37·6 +3·9	19·3* −5·4	0·6 +0·2	Held by Geoffrey Finsberg for the Conservatives since 1970. Not just Hampstead town but also Kilburn and West Hampstead. Hence this constituency is high on both professional qualifications and no baths!
Cannock and Burntwood	2,689 4·9%	Lab	Con	Con	44·5 +3·5	39·5 +2·6	16·0 −6·1		Labour failed to regain this seat in 1987 after a surprise Conservative gain in 1983. Predominantly skilled workers in light industry, plus some mining tradition.
Darlington	2,661 5·0%	Lab	Con	Con	46·6 +2·0	41·6 +3·8	11·8 −5·6		Ossie O'Brien held this seat briefly for Labour after the 1983 by-election. Few Alliance voters left for Labour to squeeze. Based on light industry, high owner-occupation. The Conservatives' only seat in Durham.

Table 1.5 —contd

Constituency	Majority over Labour 1987	Winner 1979 (Notional) 1983	Winner 1987	1987 Result (%) change since 1983 Con	Lab	Alliance (*SDP)	Other(s)	Comment
Warwickshire North	2,829 5·0%	Lab	Con	Con	45·1 +3·1	40·1 +3·0	14·8* −6·1		The Conservatives gained as much as Labour from the Alliance drop in 1987. Like many West Midlands marginals, this is still a predominantly working-class (though home-owning) seat.
Pendle	2,639 5·1%	Con	Con	Con	40·4 −3·9	35·3 +3·0	24·3 +0·9		A traditional Lancashire marginal complicated by the Liberal presence. The old Nelson and Colne seat. Many skilled workers and home-owners.
Bury South	2,679 5·2%	Con	Con	Con	46·1 +2·0	40·9 +4·4	13·1* −6·5		This is an average constituency with above-average home ownership.
Basildon	2,649 5·3%	Lab	Con	Con	43·5 +4·9	38·3 +2·6	18·2 −7·5		A substantial increase in the Conservative vote harmed Labour's chances in this Essex seat in 1987. A transformation from 1979 when Labour 'won' over half the vote. So much for New Towns ...
Rochdale	2,779 5·4%	Lib	Lib	Lib	18·6 −3·7	38·0 +7·9	43·4 −2·7		The next election will surely show that much of Cyril Smith's Liberal vote was personal.

Constituency	Majority					Vote % (change)			
Brecon and Radnor	2,329 *5.6%*	Con	Con	Con	Lib	34.7 *−13.5*	29.2 *+4.2*	34.8 *+10.5*	1.3 *−0.4*
Streatham	2,407 *5.7%*	Con	Con	Con	Con	44.9 *−1.6*	39.2 *+7.7*	15.8 *−5.4*	
Greenwich	2,141 *5.7%*	Lab	Lab	Lab	SDP	23.3 *−11.5*	34.9 *−3.4*	40.6* *+15.5*	1.3 *−0.5*
Birmingham, Northfield	3,135 *5.9%*	Con	Con	Con		45.1 *+2.4*	39.2 *+1.7*	15.6* *−3.4*	
Birmingham, Yardley	2,522 *6.0%*	Con	Con	Con		42.6 *−0.6*	36.6 *+0.3*	20.8 *+1.3*	

Brecon and Radnor: Labour until 1979, Conservative until 1985 and Liberal since Richard Livsey's by-election victory. In 1987 Livsey led the Conservatives by 56 votes with Labour third. The highest turnout of any seat in 1987.

Streatham: Conservative since 1918 but now less safe through the addition of central Brixton. In 1987 the party did well to move Streatham this high up the list.

Greenwich: Rosie Barnes (SDP) hung on in June 1987 after her by-election victory earlier in the year. But next time Labour should surely regain its traditional hold on this predominantly working-class seat on the south bank of the Thames.

Birmingham, Northfield: Labour narrowly won a by-election here in 1982 but the Conservatives regained the seat in 1983 and slightly increased their majority in 1987. Skilled working-class whites. Includes BL's Longbridge plant.

Birmingham, Yardley: In every election since 1959 this working-class marginal has been won by whichever party went on to form the government but the next time the Conservatives could lose here and still win a majority.

Table 1.5 — contd

Constituency	Majority over Labour 1987	Winner 1979	Winner (Notional) 1983	Winner 1987	1987 Result (%) change since 1983 Con	Lab	Alliance (*SDP)	Other(s)	Comment
Stockport	2,853 6·1%	Con	Con	Con	41·4 −0·8	35·3 +6·3	22·1* −5·5	1·2 0·0	The Conservative vote stayed firm in 1987 after a gain in 1983. Labour must continue to squeeze the Alliance and hope for growing strength in the North generally.
Warrington South	3,609 6·1%	Con	Con	Con	42·0 0·0	35·9 +5·9	22·2 −5·2		The electoral arithmetic resembles Stockport's (above). Based on the old Runcorn constituency.
Coventry South West	3,210 6·2%	Con	Con	Con	43·3 −1·7	37·0 +5·1	19·7 −2·9		The most white and middle-class of Coventry's four seats. Conservative since Audrey Wise's defeat in 1979. Includes Warwick University.
Barrow and Furness	3,927 7·2%	Lab	Con	Con	46·5 +2·8	39·3 +4·6	14·2* −7·4		The Conservative vote increased again in 1987 after Albert Booth's surprise defeat in 1983. Barrow builds nuclear subs; unilateralism would cost jobs. Will the 1988 strike help Labour?
Swindon	4,857 7·2%	Lab	Con	Con	43·8 +4·7	36·6 −0·1	19·6* −4·6		Long a Labour seat, the party's vote fell from a half to a third in 1983. No recovery in 1987, perhaps due to the new Conservative incumbent. A young population in a boom area;

Constituency	Majority				Shares (% and change)				Notes
Colne Valley	4,104 7.3%	Lab	Lib	Con	36.4 +2.5	29.1 +3.3	33.4 −6.4	1.1 +0.6	The Conservatives gained this traditional Lib–Lab marginal in 1987 after Richard Wainwright had hung on despite pro-Conservative boundary changes in 1983. Labour came third again in 1987 but halved the gap on the winner. High owner occupation.
Slough	4,090 7.3%	Lab	Con	Con	46.9 +4.0	39.6 +2.7	13.4* −5.1		The Conservatives increased their majority in 1987 in this working-class seat with substantial council housing and a non-white population. A Labour seat from 1970 until 1983.
Kingswood	4,393 7.5%	Lab	Con	Con	44.9 +4.5	37.4 +0.3	17.7* −4.8		A new urban seat on Bristol's eastern edge. As in Swindon, the Alliance drop helped the Conservatives not Labour in 1987. Home-owners and skilled workers, many at Rolls-Royce.
Sherwood	4,495 7.7%	Lab	Con	Con	45.9 +4.9	38.2 −1.6	16.0* −3.3		Labour lost further ground in 1987 after the remarkable Conservative gain in 1983 in this prosperous mining area where the pits worked during the strike. UDM territory.
Southwark and Bermondsey	2,779 7.7%	Lab	Lib	Lib	12.6 −0.4	39.7 +4.8	47.4 −2.4	0.3 −2.0	Simon Hughes has won twice in general elections here for the Liberals since his initial by-election triumph in 1982. Labour committed suicide here with the Mellish/Tatchell battles (or was it media murder?).

Table 1.5 —contd

Constituency	Majority over Labour 1987	Winner 1979	Winner (Notional) 1983	Winner 1987	1987 Result (%) change since 1983 Con	Lab	Alliance (*SDP)	Other(s)	Comment
Westminster North	3,310 7.9%	Con	Con	Con	47·3 +4·1	39·5 +0·1	12·1* −3·6	1·1 −0·6	The Conservative majority doubled in 1987. A typical mixed inner London seat. Based on Arthur Latham's Paddington marginal with the addition of affluent wards such as Regent's Park.
Bristol East	4,123 8.2%	Lab	Con	Con	43·6 +3·1	35·4 −1·5	20·4 −0·8	0·6 −0·7	Where Tony Benn lost in 1983. But he never won here either and Labour lost more ground in 1987. Skilled prosperous workers.
Bolton West	4,593 8.2%	Con	Con	Con	44·3 −0·8	36·1 +4·6	19·6* −3·8		Contains Bolton's best areas and high owner occupation even in the working-class wards. In the SE of England this would be a safe Conservative seat.
Rossendale and Darwen	4,982 8.3%	Con	Con	Con	46·6 −0·5	38·3 +6·5	15·1 −6·1		An odd mixture of Darwen and Rossendale Valley. Becoming Manchester commuterland but still many skilled workers. High owner occupation.

Constituency	Majority								Notes
Edinburgh, Pentlands	3,745 *8·3%*	Con	Con	Con	38·3 *−0·9*	30·0 *+6·1*	24·5* *−4·8*	7·2 *+1·2*	Malcolm Rifkind's seat. Labour overtook the Alliance in 1987 and now needs to squeeze their vote. Includes a large council estate but owner occupation predominates.
Lewisham West	3,772 *8·3%*	Con	Lab	Con	46·2 *+2·2*	37·9 *−0·5*	15·9 *−0·9*		Seven MP's since the war: four Conservative, three Labour – the last was Christopher Price, defeated in 1983.
Feltham and Heston	5,430 *9·1%*	Con	Lab	Con	46·5 *+3·1*	37·4 *−2·0*	16·1* *+0·2*		In 1987 this working-class seat with a substantial non-white population moved further away from Labour. Russell Kerr was defeated here in 1983 after holding Feltham since 1966. Considerable employment at Heathrow airport.
Chester, City of	4,855 *9·2%*	Con	Con	Con	44·9 *−2·3*	35·6 *+7·4*	19·5 *−5·2*		Labour gained considerable ground in 1987 but this seat has always been Conservative and seems likely to remain so.
Luton South	5,115 *9·6%*	Con	Con	Con	46·2 *+4·4*	36·7 *+3·4*	17·1 *−7·8*		Another southern working-class seat where Labour's prospects are receding. Includes Vauxhall Motors and Luton airport.
Elmet	5,356 *9·8%*	Con	Con	Con	46·9 *−0·4*	37·1 *+5·3*	16·0* *−4·9*		The affluent commuters to Wetherby should normally swing this mixed seat outside Wetherby to the Conservatives. But there are council tenants and miners to offer Labour some hope.

Table 1.5 —contd

Constituency	Majority over Labour 1987	Winner			1987 Result (%) change since 1983				Comment
		1979 (National)	1983	1987	Con	Lab	Alliance (*SDP)	Other(s)	
Pembroke	5,700 10·0%	Con	Con	Con	41·0 −5·9	31·0 +1·7	26·1 +5·4	2·0 −1·2	In 1987 a swing from the Conservatives to the Alliance almost halved the Conservative majority over Labour in this rural seat. 'Little England' says Waller. Includes the working-class port of Milford Haven. A Labour seat until 1970.
Croydon North West	3,988 10·0%	Con	Con	Con	47·0 +4·7	37·0 +12·7	16·0 −15·9		Bill Pitt (remember him?) won a by-election here for the Liberals in 1981. Since then the seat has been moving back to being a Conservative-held marginal. A mixed seat with a substantial non-white population.
Calder Valley	6,045 10·2%	Con	Con	Con	43·5 −0·1	33·4 +6·4	23·1 −6·2		Labour came second in 1987 but there is still a Liberal presence in this typical Pennines seat, based on textile workers living in owner-occupied homes in small valley towns.
Nuneaton	5,655 10·3%	Lab	Con	Con	44·9 +4·4	34·6 +4·0	19·2* −8·7	1·3 +0·3	Lesley Huckfield left this traditional Labour stronghold, correctly fearing the effects of boundary changes. The SDP decline in 1987 did not cut the Conservative majority. Skilled workers and home owners.

Constituency	Majority								Notes
Harlow	5,877 *10.7%*	Lab	Con	Con	47.2 *+6.1*	36.6 *+2.3*	16.2* *-8.0*		Another New Town where the Conservatives have prospered since their 1983 gain, a working-class electorate notwithstanding.
Keighley	5,606 *10.7%*	Con	Con	Con	45.8 *+3.2*	35.0 *-2.0*	19.2 *-0.6*		Bob Cryer lost a battle royal in 1983 against another sitting MP, Conservative Gary Waller. With a new candidate in 1987 Labour's vote fell as the Liberals stayed firm after suffering a squeeze in 1983.
Ilford South	4,572 *10.9%*	Con	Con	Con	48.4 *+2.9*	37.5 *+3.2*	14.1 *-5.4*		
Lewisham East	4,814 *10.9%*	Lab	Con	Con	45.1 *+4.8*	34.2 *-1.7*	20.7* *-1.3*		
Inverness, Nairn and Lochaber	5,431 *11.5%*	Lib	Lib	Lib	23.0 *-6.8*	25.3 *+11.0*	36.8 *-9.2*	14.8 *+5.0*	
Derby North	6,325 *11.6%*	Lab	Con	Con	48.9 *+5.2*	37.2 *+0.4*	13.4 *-6.1*	0.5	
Cambridge	6,305 *11.7*	Con	Con	Con	40.0 *-1.5*	28.3 *+0.1*	30.6* *+0.9*	1.1 *+0.5*	
Dover	6,541 *11.9%*	Con	Con	Con	46.0 *-2.3*	34.1 *+3.3*	19.9* *-0.3*		
Bristol North West	6,952 *12.0%*	Con	Con	Con	46.6 *+2.7*	34.6 *+2.0*	18.8* *-4.7*		

Table 1.5 —contd

Constituency	Majority over Labour 1987	Winner			1987 Result (%) change since 1983			
		1979 (Notional)	1983	1987	Con	Lab	Alliance (*SDP)	Other(s)
Vale of Glamorgan	6,251 12·1%	Con	Con	Con	46·8 −1·3	34·7 +8·9	16·7* −7·2	1·8 −0·5
Southampton, Itchen	6,716 12·2%	Lab	Con	Con	44·3 +2·8	32·1 +5·0	23·6* −7·9	
Southampton, Test	6,954 12·3%	Con	Con	Con	45·6 +0·4	33·3 +5·2	21·2 −5·6	
Bury North	6,911 12·3%	Con	Con	Con	50·1 +4·6	37·8 −2·4	12·1 −2·2	
Lincoln	7,483 12·8%	Con	Con	Con	46·5 +0·1	33·7 +6·1	19·4* −5·6	0·4 −0·6
Mitcham and Morden	6,183 12·9%	Lab	Con	Con	48·2 +5·5	35·2 +6·4	16·6* −10·8	
Chorley	8,057 13·3%	Con	Con	Con	48·0 −0·2	34·7 +4·2	16·1 −4·2	1·2 +0·2
Leicestershire North West	7,828 13·4%	Lab	Con	Con	47·6 +3·0	34·3 +1·7	17·1 −4·5	1·0 −0·1

Hayes and Harlington	5,965 *13.7%*	Lab	Con	Con	49.2 *+8.9*	35.5 *+5.6*	15.3* *-13.7*	
Plymouth, Devonport	6,873 *13.8%*	Lab	SDP	SDP	29.3 *-4.6*	28.5 *+7.5*	42.3* *-2.1*	
South Ribble	8,430 *14.1%*	Con	Con	Con	47.2 *-1.9*	33.1 *+6.5*	19.7 *-4.6*	
Lancaster	6,453 *14.2%*	Con	Con	Con	46.7 *-3.6*	32.4 *+7.5*	19.9 *-4.5*	1.0 *+0.6*
Kensington	4,447 *14.3%*	Con	Con	Con	47.5 *+1.5*	33.2 *+3.7*	17.2* *-4.9*	2.0 *-0.4*
Putney	6,907 *14.4%*	Con	Con	Con	50.5 *+4.0*	36.1 *+0.2*	12.4 *-3.9*	1.1 *-0.2*
Eastwood	7,083 *14.4%*	Con	Con	Con	39.5 *-7.1*	25.1 *+5.0*	27.2* *-0.3*	8.2 *+2.4*
Brentford and Isleworth	7,953 *14.5%*	Con	Con	Con	47.7 *+0.3*	33.2 *+4.0*	17.5* *-4.6*	1.5 *+0.4*
Fulham	6,322 *15.0%*	Con	Con	Con	51.8 *+5.6*	36.7 *+2.7*	10.4* *-7.9*	1.1 *-0.4*
Edinburgh West	7,493 *15.2%*	Con	Con	Con	37.4 *-0.8*	22.2 *+2.0*	34.9 *-2.2*	5.6 *+1.0*

Table 1.5 —contd

Constituency	Majority over Labour 1987	Winner 1979 (Notional)	Winner 1983	Winner 1987	1987 Result (%) change since 1983 Con	Lab	Alliance (*SDP)	Other(s)
Edmonton	7,286 15·2%	Lab	Con	Con	51·2 +8·7	36·0 −3·8	12·8* −4·1	
Gravesham	8,792 15·2%	Con	Con	Con	50·1 +2·7	34·8 +2·9	15·1 −4·6	
Eltham	6,460 15·5%	Con	Con	Con	47·5 −0·4	32·0 +2·7	20·5 −1·6	
Erith and Crayford	6,994 15·6%	Lab	Con	Con	45·2 +8·1	29·5 +2·2	25·3* −9·6	
Norwich North	7,776 15·6%	Con	Con	Con	45·8 +1·2	30·2 −2·2	24·0 +1·4	
Peterborough	9,784 15·8%	Con	Con	Con	49·4 +2·3	33·6 +4·6	16·1 −6·6	0·8 −0·4
Dudley West	10,244 15·8%	Con	Con	Con	49·8 +3·7	34·0 +2·6	16·2 −6·3	
Derbyshire South	10,311 15·9%	Lab	Con	Con	49·1 +5·3	33·2 +4·0	17·7* −9·3	

| Blackpool South | 6,744 15·9% | Con | Con | Con | 48·0 −2·5 | 32·1 +7·3 | 19·9* −4·1 |

Notes

1. The 'incumbency effect' is worth up to 1,000 votes to a new MP seeking re-election for the first time.
2. A 'new seat' is one created by the redistribution of 1983.
3. By-elections (such as the SNP gain from Labour in Glasgow Govan in 1988) excluded.
4. The comments are updated from Waller (1987) and Crewe and Fox (1984).
5. The table includes eight SLD/SDP seats.
6. The 1979 'winner' is based on the BBC/ITN estimate of how the seat would have voted had it existed at that time.

these eleven North/West seats. But again, this is a longer term consideration. In 1991, barring a remarkable Conservative decline, Labour's chances in these twenty-two seats vary between remote and nil.

Characteristics of the Marginals

What, then, are the characteristics of the seats which Labour needs to win? We first review the geography of the marginals, then we look at their social characteristics.

Geographically, the target seats are quite widely spread, suggesting that Labour should aim at Britain as a whole rather than particular regions. As Figure 1.1 and Table 1.6 show, the majority of the seats Labour needs to gain run diagonally across England, from the North-West through the Midlands and into London. These three areas contain thirty-four of the top sixty and sixty of the top 100. However, excluding London, there are relatively few marginals in the South where Labour's decline has been sharpest. Only nine of the top sixty, and eighteen of the top 100, are in East Anglia, the South-West or the South-East outside London. Most seats in these areas are unwinnable for Labour and fortunately do not need to be won. In 1991, at least, Labour can in theory put together a Commons majority from its

Table 1.6 Regional Distribution of Marginal Seats

	Top 60	Top 100	All seats (GB)
South-East (except London)	5	9	108 (17%)
Greater London	10	24	84 (13%)
South-West	3	5	48 (8%)
East Anglia	1	4	20 (3%)
East Midlands	4	8	42 (7%)
West Midlands	8	9	58 (9%)
Yorkshire & Humberside	6	6	54 (9%)
North-West	12	19	73 (12%)
North	5	5	36 (6%)
Wales	3	5	38 (6%)
Scotland	3	6	72 (11%)
	60	100	633

Figure 1.1 The Top Sixty Con–Lab Marginals

bases in Scotland, Wales and Northern England, combined with a superb performance in the Midlands and London.

The need for Labour to develop a wide-ranging appeal is confirmed by social and economic analyses of the marginals. Labour's target seats are spread across most types of constituency when seats are grouped by socio-economic characteristics (for details of the classification used, see Crewe and Fox, 1984). The marginals are slightly concentrated in four types which account for twenty-four of the top sixty (40 per cent) but only 16 per cent of all seats. However, even these seats are distinctive only by their normality. They are: 'intermediate industrial areas' (e.g. Darlington); 'textile areas' (e.g. Batley & Spen); 'city constituencies with service employment' (e.g. Birmingham Selly Oak); and 'metropolitan industrial areas' (e.g. Basildon). Overall, the variety of economic bases in the target seats suggests an appeal by Labour to sectoral interests would be fruitless. A better strategy is to concentrate on demonstrating overall economic competence.

We also examined the social character of the target seats using the 1981 census and more recent figures for unemployment and density of the electorate. (Although the census figures are out of date, the general pattern they reveal will still apply.) In general, this analysis supported the thesis of the representative nature of the marginals. As Table 1.7 shows, the averages for the target seats are very close to those for all constituencies. In addition, and perhaps more surprisingly, the variations around these averages are not very much less for the marginals than for all seats. That is, the marginals are not a set of average seats but a group which forms a fairly representative sample of all seats. The figures for the marginals are certainly closer to those for the country as a whole than they are to Labour's existing seats. On average, as the table shows, Labour's target seats contain appreciably more white-collar households, home-owners and car-owners than the constituencies Labour currently represents.

The politically important exception to the representative character of the target seats is the urban nature of those in South/East Britain. Over 70 per cent of these qualify as 'very urban' or 'inner city' seats. So Labour's performance in the cities of the South and Midlands, especially London, is critical. Labour's task in the capital is made more difficult by economic prosperity and population trends (the overall decline in London's population

Table 1.7 Social Characteristics of the Target Seats (Mean percentages for each type of seat)

	All seats	'Top 60'	Target seats in North/ West	in South/ East	Labour seats
(Number of seats)	(633)	(60)	(29)	(31)	(229)
Professional and managerial households	17.7	16.1	17.6	14.8	11.5
Manual households	45.5	47.2	46.2	48.0	52.4
Unemployed as per cent of electorate (July 1988)	5.4	5.9	5.7	6.0	8.1
Households owner occupied	55.0	56.5	64.2	49.3	43.2
Households with car	60.2	58.3	59.8	56.9	48.7
Density (electors per hectare) (1988)	14.9	20.3	10.5	29.5	20.3

Note: Analysis based on the 1981 census except where indicated.

has virtually stopped and a small increase is projected by the end of the century. Also, as is well known, the rich are populating some areas which have long been the home to mainly working-class people). Nevertheless, Labour simply cannot afford a repeat of 1987 when it lost two London seats to the Conservatives.

Statistically, there is also a big difference between the North/ West and South/East marginals in terms of housing. Home-ownership is higher in target seats in the North/West than the South/East. However, the marginals in the South/East are not naturally better territory just because they have more council tenants. Labour does better in all social groups in the North/ West. So despite the apparently less favourable social character of the marginals in this region, Labour has as much chance of capturing them as the targets in the South/East.

In general, then, the target seats can be regarded as a broad cross-section of Britain. So Labour's appeal should be wide and general rather than finely targeted. In the next chapter we show that this point can be applied to voters as well as constituencies.

Chapter 2
Votes

What then are the prospects of Labour achieving the lead it is likely to need for victory in 1991? More realistically, can Labour restrict the Conservative lead so as to produce a hung Parliament? We examine here three issues which bear directly on these questions:

1. What is the underlying level of support for Labour and how firm is it? This will establish the size of the base from which Labour has to build. Our answer is about 35 per cent with 20 per cent as the absolutely solid core. There is substantial evidence of a natural Conservative lead.

2. How many votes are 'up for grabs' and which parties are competing for them? This will establish how far Labour can hope to advance beyond its base within current alignments. Our answer is not far enough. Labour can make significant progress among 'open voters' but decisive progress will require detaching supporters from other parties.

3. What are the social characteristics and political attitudes of the target voters who are most likely to switch to Labour? This will establish how Labour should pitch its appeal. Our answer is that the target voters are socially and attitudinally representative of the electorate as a whole; the target group is the electorate. Labour would therefore be well advised to emphasise its general strengths rather than launch specialised appeals to particular groups.

What Is the Underlying Support for Labour?

The sad tale of Labour's decline at general elections is shown in Table 2.1. Commentary is hardly needed, but note that part of

Table 2.1 General Election Results: Share of the Vote, Great Britain, 1959–87

Year of election	Conservative %	Labour %	Liberal/ Alliance %	Liberal vote per candidate (UK) %	Number of Liberal candidates
1959	48.8	44.6	6.0	16.9	216
1964	42.9	44.8	11.4	18.5	365
1966	41.4	48.9	8.6	16.1	311
1970	46.2	43.9	7.6	13.5	322
Feb 1974	38.8	38.0	19.8	23.6	517
Oct 1974	36.7	40.2	18.8	18.9	619
1979	44.9	37.8	14.1	14.9	577
1983	43.5	28.3	26.0	26.0	633
1987	43.3	31.5	23.1	23.1	633

the fall up to October 1974 was due to an increasing number of Liberal candidates. In that election the Liberals fielded virtually a full slate, so none of the far greater decline since then can be attributed to this factor. Also, it is unwise to assume that Labour could never do worse than the 28 per cent recorded in 1983. During that campaign nearly 30 per cent of Labour voters considered voting for another party!

To fill out the picture of Labour's performance, we look first at the annual averages of Gallup's monthly polls of voting intentions (Table 2.2). Along with all the other regular polls, these also show a sharp decline in Labour's support in the 1980s. Not since 1980 has Labour's annual average in Gallup or MORI reached 40 per cent. In 1989, Labour may well break through the 40 per cent barrier but not necessarily with the lead needed for a majority at the next election.

Another measure of underlying support for Labour is party identification. The question used is: 'Generally speaking, do you usually think of yourself as Conservative, Labour, Liberal, (Social Democrat, Nationalist) or what?' A second attempt is

Table 2.2 Averages of Gallup's Monthly Polls of Voting Intentions

	Conserv-ative %	Labour	Liberal/ Alliance/ SLD + SDP	Conservative lead over Labour
1945–49	40	44	12	− 4
1950–59	44	46	9	− 2
1960–69	42	42	12	
1970–79	42	43	11	− 1
1980	37	45	14	− 8
1981	30	35	32	− 5
1982	38	30	29	+ 8
1983	43	30	23	+13
1984	40	35	22	+ 5
1985	32	35	31	− 3
1986	32	37	29	− 5
1987	42	34	22	+ 8
1988	44	37	16	+ 7
1989 (Jan–June)	40	39	15	+ 1

Note: Since 1980 Labour's annual average in MORI's polls has been between 0.5 and 2.7 points higher than in Gallup's. The mean annual difference is 1.4 points.

made to establish an identification for those who do not name a party: 'Do you generally think of yourself as a little closer to one of the parties than the others?' Those expressing an allegiance are then asked how strong it is. Table 2.3 gives figures for party identification since 1964.

Table 2.3 Party Identification, 1964–87

LEVEL OF IDENTIFICATION

	Conservative	Labour	Liberal/ SDP/ Alliance	Conservative lead over Labour
	%			
British Election Studies				
1964	42	45	13	− 3
1966	39	50	11	−11
1970	44	47	8	− 3
Feb 1974	39	45	14	− 6
Oct 1974	38	44	16	− 6
1979	44	42	13	+ 2
1983	43	35	20	+ 8
BBC/Gallup				
1983	42	37	19	+ 5
1987	43	36	19	+ 7

STRENGTH OF IDENTIFICATION

	Labour			Conservative		
	Very strong %	*Fairly strong*	*Not very strong*	*Very strong* %	*Fairly strong*	*Not very strong*
British Election Studies						
1964	49	37	13	47	39	13
1966	48	39	13	47	37	16
1970	45	38	17	48	38	14
Feb 1974	38	41	21	31	47	22
Oct 1974	35	46	19	26	51	23
1979	27	48	26	22	51	27
1983	27	38	35	23	43	33
BBC/Gallup						
1983	31	38	31	32	41	27
1987	36	38	26	30	43	27

Base: All identifiers.
Note: The BBC/Gallup data were reweighted to produce a distribution of votes which matched the actual election results.

In the 1960s and 1970s Labour's identification level averaged 45 per cent and varied only slightly. Even when Labour's vote dropped by six points in response to the Liberal revival in February 1974, identification with Labour did not fall significantly. In 1979, the level recorded was only three points lower than 1964, though Labour's long-held advantage on this measure had disappeared. So after all the electoral turmoil of the 1970s, the post-war politics of a battle for power between two fairly evenly matched parties remained the underlying reality.

By 1983 this had changed. A nine point fall in Labour's vote was accompanied by a seven point drop in party identification, down to 35 per cent. For the first time the Conservatives had a substantial lead in party allegiance. Labour was punished not just with a huge loss of votes but also with a sizable reduction in general support.

Figures for strength of identification confirmed the seriousness of this loss of support for Labour. The proportion of Labour identifiers with a 'very strong' or 'fairly strong' allegiance fell by ten points between 1979 and 1983. Conservative support, too, had become less strongly attached. But the combination of reduced and weaker support was specific to Labour. It resulted in a fall in the proportion of strong Labour identifiers in the electorate from over a fifth in 1964 to under a tenth in 1983! Labour did not retreat into a solid base of hardcore support, as one might have thought. Instead, this base shrank dramatically.

In 1987, Labour managed to stabilise the position but not to recover support. The party got more votes largely because more Labour identifiers voted for it. In 1983, only 74 per cent of Labour identifiers who said they would definitely vote reported they would vote Labour. In 1987, this figure was a much more creditable 83 per cent. Labour will do well to gain more than a couple of extra points from its identifiers. For it is notable that Labour's vote has never exceeded its identification level. Why is not clear, but the identification level appears to be an upper limit for Labour rather than an indicator of the share of the vote the party can expect to achieve. This means that Labour's 'natural vote' in 1987 was more like 34 per cent than the 36 per cent shown in the party identification table. So Labour hardly 'underpolled' at all in 1987 – at most by three percentage points. The main problem is that Labour's base remains far below the level of support needed to win.

Keep Britain Labour.

Published by the Labour Party, Transport House,
Smith Square, London SW1P 3JA.

The poster was the work of John O'Driscoll, Caroline Bard, and Tim Delaney

This innovative poster was caught up in Labour party politics in 1979 and was not used in the campaign. Fortunately, advertising skills are more widely appreciated in today's Labour Party.

It is instructive to compare Labour's position with that of socialist parties abroad. Table 2.4 shows the level and recent trend in the vote for ten left-wing, non-communist parties. The table excludes Italy and France, where communist parties intrude, and Greece, Portugal and Spain, where socialists were successfully linked to new modernising regimes. With these countries removed, the average vote for the major left-wing party at the most recent election was 38 per cent. If we remove Australia, New Zealand and Sweden, where the left has benefited from incumbency, the average falls to 35 per cent – in line with all the other evidence about Labour's natural vote.

It is true that the left vote has fallen more sharply in Britain than elsewhere. Most left parties are performing below their post-war average but Labour's decline has been exceptionally severe. This suggests that Labour should not have fallen as far behind as it has but does not mean that there is a huge reservoir of lost Labour supporters waiting to be rediscovered. Labour continues to pay the price for its failures in the past, especially those of the late 1970s and early 1980s. These political difficulties have cut Labour's underlying support to the mid-thirties. Yet decline is not irreversible – there remains the hope of expanding support through political action. We turn, then, to examine just how many extra votes are available for Labour to win.

How Many Votes Are Up for Grabs?

There is a good deal of openness among the electorate, but this is not a new phenomenon. Past volatility is generally underestimated because much of the switching by individual voters cancelled out, yielding an overall but misleading image of stability. Recent evidence suggests little, if any, increase in individual volatility since 1966 (Heath *et al.*, 1988). If weakening identification suggests that greater volatility is likely, then the recent polarisation of the two main parties may well be a force for increased stability. The vast majority of the electorate – over 80 per cent – now believes there is a great deal of difference between the Conservative and Labour parties. In contrast, in each election survey between 1964 and 1979 less than 45 per cent thought this was the case. It is therefore wrong to assume that *growing* volatility will make it easier for Labour to gain large

Table 2.4 Percentage Vote for Major Left-wing, Non-communist Parties

Country	Party	Mean vote 1950–88 %	Most recent election Vote %	Most recent election Year	Most recent vote minus mean post-war vote
Australia	Labour	45.2	45.8	1987	+0.6
Austria	Socialist	46.1	43.1	1986	−3.0
Denmark	Social Democrats	36.2	29.3	1987	−6.9
Finland	Social Democrats	24.7	24.1	1987	−0.6
Germany	Social Democrats	38.3	34.5	1987	−3.8
Netherlands	Labour	29.2	33.3	1986	+4.1
New Zealand	Labour	43.8	48.0	1987	+4.2
Norway	Labour	43.0	41.2	1985	−1.8
Sweden	Social Democrats	45.6	44.7	1985	−0.9
UNITED KINGDOM	LABOUR	41.0	30.8	1987	−10.2

Sources: calculated from Mackie and Rose (1982) and annual updates in the *European Journal of Political Research.*
Note: For more detailed figures see Crewe (1989).

numbers of extra votes. But just how many votes are genuinely up for grabs and which parties are competing for them?

To estimate this we develop a model based on two types of voters: 'party loyalists' who will almost certainly only vote for one particular party and 'open voters' who will seriously consider more than one party. The balance between these types cannot be established precisely. One problem is deciding what degree of certainty makes someone a loyalist; another is lack of data specifically measuring this dichotomy. So it should be borne in mind that our model is an estimation and, of course, that the figures can change over time. Nevertheless, we confidently suggest that party loyalists are a majority of the electorate. The evidence for this judgement includes the following:

● When voters were asked in July 1987 about how they expected to vote in the next election, 55 per cent said that they would definitely vote for the same party. (We doubt that all loyalists would give this response, as some might think it unwise to say that a party is assured of their vote no matter what it does. So a higher figure for loyalists is consistent with this finding.)

● In 1987, according to Gallup, 80 per cent of voters said they had decided how to vote 'a long time ago', rather than during the campaign.

● Of voters interviewed for the 1987 British Election Study, only just over a quarter said that they had seriously thought, during the campaign, that they might vote for another party (Heath, Jowell and Curtice, 1988).

● 71 per cent of 1983 voters reinterviewed in 1986 and 1987 for the Election Study panel supported the same party on all three occasions.

● Of a sample of some 400 people interviewed in 1983, 1984, 1985 and 1986 for the British Social Attitudes panel only 30 per cent changed the party they supported.

So the data indicate that somewhere between 55 and 70 per cent of voters are loyalists. Our estimate is 58 per cent, towards the lower end of this range, since without firm evidence we would not want to imply that the proportion of loyalists was a good

Labour needs to recreate the sense of moving forward which was apparent in 1964.

deal higher than the proportion who said that they would definitely vote the same way next time. Also, the figures from panel surveys refer only to how many people changed allegiance, not to how many considered doing so. Thus they may suggest too high a figure for loyalists. Breakdowns of the data by party show that loyalists are divided between the Conservative, Labour and centre parties roughly in the ratio 30:20:10. This, though, is being a little generous to the centre parties, who probably have the loyal support of only about 8 per cent of voters. As Table 2.5 shows, this means that we settle on a figure of 58 per cent for 'loyalists' and, thus, 42 per cent for 'open voters'.

Table 2.5   A Model of the Electorate: Party Loyalists and Open Voters, 1987

Party loyalists		*Open voters*	
Conservative loyalists	30%	Between Conservative and 'centre'	17%
Labour loyalists	20%	Between Labour and 'centre'	17%
Centre party loyalists	8%	Between Conservative and Labour	4.5%
		Between all three	3.5%
Total loyalists	58%	Total open voters	42%

Note: This model predates the emergence of the Greens. They can be allocated to the centre for the purposes of the model.

Of course, these 'open' voters are not 'open' to all parties. The numbers deciding between the Conservatives and the centre party(ies), on the one hand, and Labour and the centre, on the other, appear to be similar, though there may be slightly more in the former category. The group which considers only Conservative and Labour is much smaller – only about a quarter the size of each of the above groups. The number genuinely considering all the contending parties is probably smaller still. On this basis we can put figures to the categories of open voters. We must note, though, that these are more speculative and probably more fluid than either the division between loyalists and open voters or the party distribution of loyalists.

The model implies the following ranges for each party:

Conservative	30%–55%
Labour	20%–45%
SLD + SDP	8%–45%

However, it is very unlikely that any party will finish close to either extreme. In particular, Labour could only get near to the top of its range if both the Conservatives and the centre parties made a complete mess of it. Incompetence by the centre parties alone could help Labour into the high thirties – and the Conservatives into the high forties! If the other parties perform adequately Labour will do well to pick up much above fourteen points from open voters and, thus, 34 per cent in total. Not surprisingly, this ties in with what the party identification measure suggests Labour might achieve as long as political, economic and social circumstances are much as they were in 1987.

The main conclusion from the model, then, is that Labour needs to go beyond simply winning more of the votes for which it currently competes. Labour needs an expansion of the potential share of the vote available to it. In theory this can be done without winning over supporters of other parties. For there is considerable movement in and out of voting due to (i) abstentions and (ii) death and coming of age, and also (iii) emigration and immigration. This turnover has affected party support in the past. In the 1960s and 1970s it altered the gap between the major parties from one election to the next by up to 3 per cent, with no party consistently favoured. Labour could, therefore, increase its share of the vote by persuading more of its supporters to turn out and vote (as long as the other parties did not do likewise). Capturing a very high proportion of first time voters would also help, though there will be fewer of these in 1991 than in recent elections. Neither objective should be neglected, but both will be difficult to achieve. In any case, in practice they could deliver only a small proportion of the extra votes required.

Therefore, what Labour really needs is for more people to consider voting for the party. Short-term improvements in Labour's poll ratings do not necessarily show that Labour's potential support has increased. 'Votes' may be gained without more people considering Labour. For example, extra support derived from centre party incompetence may well mean that Labour picks up more open voters, not that the numbers considering a Labour vote have increased significantly. By mid-1989 the proportion considering a Labour vote may have increased slightly but there is still far to go before a large number of extra votes are secured. So what are the characteristics of those most likely to be won over?

Who Are the Target Voters?

Target voters are often defined ideologically, as those people whose interests Labour specifically seeks to represent and who might therefore be expected to share Labour's values and priorities. In this sense, the working class and council tenants are target voters. But we prefer a more pragmatic definition. We define target voters as those whom Labour is most able to recruit, irrespective of their social position. In our definition, target voters are non-Labour electors who are considering voting Labour or who might be persuaded more easily than most to consider a Labour vote. For example: those who did not vote Labour in 1987 but who said they thought of doing so or at least retained a general loyalty to the party.

Target voters are not easy to measure but however they are identified we emerge with the same conclusion as Mark Abrams (1964) twenty-five years ago: *In terms of social characteristics and even political attitudes, Labour's target voters are broadly representative of the electorate as a whole.* So, in general terms, Labour can identify what its target voters are thinking simply by looking at the views of the whole electorate.

We list below some (by no means all) of the target groups we have examined:

1. Those who identified with Labour in 1987 but voted for another party.

   Size: 6 per cent of all voters.

   Characteristics: As Table 2.6 shows, Labour's prosperity rating was very poor and unilateral nuclear disarmament very unpopular among this group. Otherwise Labour's ratings were none too bad and faith in the Alliance was

Table 2.6 Labour Identifiers Who Did Not Vote Labour in 1987 Compared with Labour Voters and the Electorate as a Whole

	Labour identifiers who did not vote Labour %	*Labour voters* %	*All electors* %
Best party at reducing unemployment			
Conservative	23	2	30
Labour	44	96	41
Alliance	18	1	11
Best party at making Britain more prosperous			
Conservative	48	14	52
Labour	15	71	23
Alliance	21	3	12
Cut taxes or keep up services?			
Cut taxes	14	7	12
Keep up services	85	90	84
Nuclear weapons			
Keep Trident	29	13	39
Minimal nuclear deterrent	52	39	37
Get rid of all nuclear weapons	14	43	18
Trade union membership			
Yes (self or husband)	51	42	32
No	47	56	67
Housing			
Owns	69	47	63
Rents from council	20	42	26
Rents privately	10	10	10
Class (head of household)			
Professional	10	7	11
Director, proprietor, manager	13	5	12
Office, shop, student, etc.	13	16	19
Skilled manual	39	36	33
Semi- and unskilled manual	26	36	25

Source: BBC/Gallup, 1987.

remarkably limited. Figures for the working class and union membership are higher than in the whole electorate. Good potential for Labour to win votes here provided it can improve on defence and the economy. However, note the size of the group – to win Labour needs many more extra votes than are available here.

2. Alliance voters in 1987 who identified with no party or identified only weakly with the 'Alliance' or the Conservative Party.

Size: 7 per cent of voters.

Characteristics: Even less faith in Labour on defence and prosperity among this group. The Alliance did best on Labour's natural issues of jobs and the public services. Larger middle class than in group 1. This group looks more difficult for Labour.

3. Alliance and Conservative identifiers who are no more hostile to Labour than to the Conservatives (on a scale rating each party from 'very strongly in favour' to 'very strongly against').

Size: 16 per cent of all identifiers.

Characteristics: Labour was a long way behind on unity among this sizable group though more rated the Conservatives as extreme. This group is a social cross-section of the electorate apart from an overrepresentation of home-owners. On most policy issues there are slightly more left-wing responses than among the whole electorate – especially, for example, in the numbers favouring (a) increased taxes and more spending on services and (b) less government control of local authorities.

Two specific points to note from this analysis are cases where majority characteristics of the whole electorate are even more strongly represented in the target groups. The first is lack of support for Labour on the economy and defence. Persuading every one of the unilateralists in the target groups to vote Labour would increase Labour's total vote only slightly. To appeal successfully to the majority of these target voters, Labour has to convince them of the merits of unilateralism, persuade them to vote Labour despite their objections, or change its policy.

Secondly, we find high levels of home ownership among the target voters. Over 70 per cent of groups 2 and 3 own their homes compared to about half of Labour's voters. So both to secure and expand support, Labour will need to be sure that home-owners do not regard Labour as a threat to the benefits attached to ownership.

The overall picture is that the target voters are a broadly representative section of the whole electorate. This implies that Labour must seek to improve its performance among nearly all sections of society. There is no large bloc of votes which has temporarily defected from Labour because of the party's short-term performance and which can quickly be regained through effective campaigning. Nor is an appeal targeted on specific groups on the basis of sectional interest likely to bring sufficient, or even many, extra votes. Instead Labour will have to appeal to general interests by showing general skills. In particular it will have to demonstrate over a sustained period that it is fit and ready to govern. In the next two chapters we examine specific issues of image and policy related to this.

It would be unwise to conclude this chapter by suggesting a precise figure which the party might hope to achieve in 1991. Like all oppositions, Labour's chances depend greatly on factors outside its control – many of which are controlled by the government. If the centre remains weak, Labour can expect a substantial improvement on its 1987 performance but the Conservatives could also benefit from the weakness of the Democrats. The lead Labour requires still looks elusive.

Part II

Requirements

Chapter 3
Competence

In contrast to firms supplying products, political parties offer a service – the service of governing the country. This means that Tony Benn is quite right to say that parties cannot be marketed like washing powder. But he is wrong to conclude that parties cannot be marketed at all. Since Labour is inevitably competing for votes, it has to market itself and always has done. Its marketing is simply the way it seeks to secure votes. Our proposition is that Labour's marketing must be based on presenting the party for what it is – a potential supplier of the *service* of governing. By reviewing the three main features of this service, we can establish the principal requirements of the market in which the Labour Party operates.

First, governing, like other services, is contracted for in advance of supply. Services are sold then delivered whereas goods are produced then sold. Thus services must inevitably depend on faith – the belief that the supplier will offer future satisfaction. This means that the Labour Party, like any other service organisation, must project competence, credibility and reliability. If the party seeks commercial inspiration, the model should be service organisations like the Halifax Building Society, not products like Daz and Omo. Above all the party must emphasise delivered-quality – what it will achieve in office. This is far more important than designed-quality – what the party promises in its manifesto.

Second, governments provide a wide range of services. Indeed the precise services to be provided cannot be identified in advance. Who predicted the Arab oil crisis or the Falklands? So it is essential to instil faith in the party's ability to seize unexpected opportunities and handle unanticipated threats. This has to be achieved through the party's leaders. Not only do they deliver the service but in common with any other organisation supplying intangible services the suppliers personify the service. Labour's leaders should aim to be well-regarded general managers.

Third, there is only one supplier of government at a time. The Conservatives can project competence by being competent; Labour can only do so by claiming competence. Not surprisingly, in this situation people tend to judge the current supplier first. It is only when governments fail that people look seriously at oppositions – and oppositions are judged by their history as well as their rhetoric. Labour's past failures in office therefore remain influential. The party needs to distance itself from these and convince people that it should be judged anew.

So the requirements of the electoral market are plain enough. Because governing is a service, Labour must convey credibility and competence. Because governments provide a range of services, Labour's leaders must convey general authority. And because Labour is not the current supplier, it needs a strategy for winning from opposition despite its own past failures. Reviewing public opinion about the Labour Party in each of these areas reveals the depth of Labour's difficulties, and very few clues about how to overcome them.

Credibility and Competence

Currently, Labour scores well below the Conservatives on ability to govern. For example:

How competent do you think the . . . Party is to manage the country's affairs? November 1988

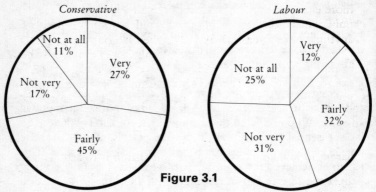

Figure 3.1

Note: Don't knows (5%) excluded. The Gallup survey from which these questions are taken showed a six-point Conservative lead in voting intentions.

So only four in ten electors believe that Labour is at least fairly competent to manage the country's affairs (most of whom intend to vote Labour anyway), compared with eight in ten who think this of the Conservatives. This is a huge credibility gap which Labour simply has to close. Perceived competence is a prerequisite of electoral success. Non-Labour voters sympathetic to Labour's philosophy will not switch to the party unless they believe that Labour can govern satisfactorily.

Doubts about Labour's governing ability stem from recent history. At the end of each year Gallup asks, 'So far as you are concerned, do you think that 19 . . (next year) will be better or worse than 19 . . (last year)?' Under the last Labour administration, pessimists exceeded optimists every year except 1977. By contrast, under the Conservatives, optimists have outnumbered pessimists every year since 1981. Not since the Macmillan era has any government presided over such optimistic times. The blunt fact is that things have gone better with the Conservatives. Labour must indeed offer more than the personal well-being referred to in Gallup's question but equally Labour must not threaten that well-being.

Competence ratings distil all the crucial elements of a party's image – the coherence of its policies, the effectiveness of its leaders, evaluations of its record in office. But one particularly strong influence on competence must surely be unity. Electors may not expect all members of a party to agree on everything but they certainly do expect the leader to control the party and to lead a team united behind key objectives. How then does Labour rate on unity? As Figure 3.2 shows, throughout the 1980s many more electors have viewed Labour as divided than united. The public image of the two big parties differs more on unity than anything else. Even in May 1989, when Labour had caught the Conservatives on voting intentions, only 22 per cent saw Labour as united (Conservatives, 59 per cent). Yet, as the figure also shows, Labour has not always been behind the Conservatives on this unity measure. The two parties were closely matched in 1974. And back in the 1960s Labour was ahead on unity. There is nothing inherent in the party which means that it must always be perceived as divided. The difficulty seems to be that it is much harder to lose an unfavourable image than it is to acquire one – yet the Figure suggests Labour must somehow catch the Conservatives on perceived unity if it is to win the next election.

Is the . . . Party united or divided at the present time?

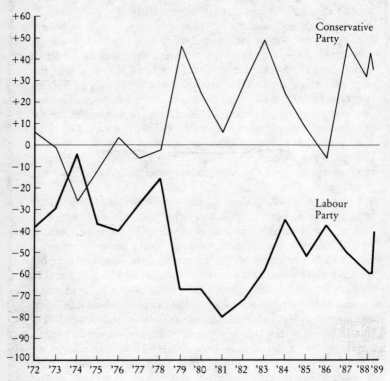

Note: Percentage saying party is united; minus percentage saying divided.
Source: Gallup

Figure 3.2 Unity Index

Cummings

YOU CAN TRUST MR ATTLEE

Reproduced by permission of the Daily Express.

The 'loony left' is an old theme. This cartoon of Attlee and Nye Bevan is from 1955.

The Conservatives' own record is patchy: remarkable success at projecting unity in the last three election campaigns but otherwise there has been some awareness of divisions within the Conservative camp. The problem is more Labour's disunity than Conservative unity. Generally, more voters prefer a united party which divides the country (the Conservatives) to a divided party which seeks to unite the country (Labour).

A second influence on competence is moderation. Moderate parties are more likely than extreme parties to be seen as competent. In fact Labour's ratings here, though poor in absolute terms, are little worse than the Conservatives'. Table 3.1 reveals a significant improvement after 1983 in Labour's perceived moderation – greater than on unity – followed by a sharp deterioration in the year up to the 1987 election as the 'loony left' campaign had an effect. However, since 1987 ratings of Labour as extreme have again declined. The problem here is not that more people see Labour than the Conservatives as extreme but that an extremist image seems to put more people off Labour than the Conservatives. It would surely be prudent for Labour to position itself not necessarily as moderate, but at least as radical rather than extreme.

Table 3.1 Would you describe the ... Party nowadays as extreme or moderate?

| | Conservative | | | | Labour | | | |
	1983	1984	1986	1987	1983	1984	1986	1987
Extreme (%)	48	48	54	44	49	41	39	51
Moderate (%)	40	37	35	44	37	41	46	37

Source: BSA, BES.

However, the key is for Labour to improve its competence ratings. And the basis of that is unity.

Leadership

The service of government is delivered by political leaders. They must symbolise the competence and trustworthiness of their party. How do Labour's leaders rate?

Since 1979 the voters have consistently rated the Conservative Party as having the best leaders and often by a spectacular margin. In the 1980s, Labour's leadership deficit has consistently exceeded its policy deficit. Even in May 1989, when the Conservative lead in voting intentions had disappeared, the Conservatives were still rated as the party with the best leaders by 56 per cent of electors. Only 22 per cent chose Labour.

Neil Kinnock's personal ratings have been none too bad. The proportion of the electorate saying he is proving a good leader of his party (1983–7 average: 40 per cent, 1987–8 average: 35 per cent) is similar to the ratings of both Heath (33 per cent) and Thatcher (41 per cent) before their victories from opposition in the 1970s. Kinnock's ratings are, however, well below those achieved by Harold Wilson before his wins in 1964 (1963–4 average: 59 per cent) and February 1974 (1970–4 average: 49 per cent).

The real problem is not the level of Neil Kinnock's popularity but the nature of his image. Like his party, indeed partly because of his party, Neil Kinnock is perceived as caring, concerned and even likable. But again like the party, he rates poorly on ability to govern. Margaret Thatcher's image is exactly the reverse: cold and inflexible but also strong, determined and, of course, experienced. Unfortunately for Labour, the capacity to govern effectively is what people look for first. In 1985, Gallup found that voters rated 'has a clear view and purpose of the future of the country' one of the main requirements for a Prime Minister. In the same year, Harris found 'a strong character' and 'sticks to their guns' to be important features of the ideal leader. On all these dimensions Thatcher scores highly. Kinnock's lead is largely confined to softer, less essential qualities: for example 'compassionate' or – least important of all – 'has a happy home life'. It is not that Kinnock's caring virtues are irrelevant. Rather they will only become relevant when added to a foundation of skill at governing.

Demonstrating leadership ability in opposition is never easy, especially when the party has been out of office for twelve years and there is opposition within as well as without. (Kinnock is not the first Labour leader to note that in comparison with Labour 'at any time in history the Tory party could be run by the average Labour leader in his spare time'.) It is impossible to be a strong leader of a divided party. Another leader would be an

Which party has the best leaders and best policies?

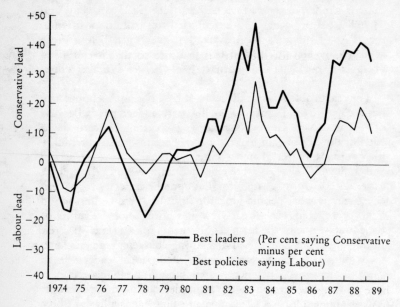

Source: Gallup

Figure 3.3 Leaders

improvement only if he or she could better organise the party so as to demonstrate strength and the ability to get things done.

As Rita Hinden noted in 1960 (in Abrams and Rose, 1960) there is a danger of the party blaming the leader for its own failings:

> It would be quite wrong to see this as the failure of one particular man, and to deceive ourselves into thinking that someone else might have had plain sailing. Although another leader might have tackled problems differently, he would have encountered resistance too. The difficulty lies in the very nature of a party of ideals, as the Labour Party is; it is exacerbated by the present confused state of socialism itself.

The real message for the party is to unite so that it can give priority to the requirements of the electoral market when selecting its leader in the first place.

None the less, Labour does need to project its leader as a sharper, more decisive figure. It must show that its leadership team as a whole is competent and confident. But above all it must unite so that the leader is seen as capable of running his own organisation.

Winning from Opposition

At the next election Labour faces the unenviable task of convincing the electorate it can supply a service it has not supplied for twelve years. Oppositions do have some advantages, of course. They can attack the incumbent's record, they have no recent record of their own to defend, they find it easier to present new ideas and a fresh image, and they can claim to be closer to the people. But essentially marketing opposition parties always means exploiting opportunities, not creating them. Labour can only win the next election by helping the government to lose it.

So what opportunities are there for the Labour Party to exploit? Governments lose in several circumstances: (a) when they fail completely, (b) when they run out of steam, or (c) when they succeed too well.

(a) At first sight there would seem to be little prospect of the Conservative government failing completely. After all,

Thatcher's main achievement has been to restore the power of government over sectional interests. But only a brave soul would predict the era of high inflation, burgeoning interest rates and swelling imports has gone for good. The grumblings of the British economy may bring chances for Labour still. Labour will need detailed, credible policies for improving economic performance if the Conservatives are seen to be failing here by the next election.

(b) Nor would there seem to be much chance of the Conservatives running out of steam. Mrs Thatcher's reforming zeal continues unabated. The main chance for Labour here will be if the Conservatives propose increasingly hare-brained schemes in their attempt to avoid looking tired. What can they privatise if only the security forces are left? How much further can welfare provision be rolled back? Although there are few precedents for British governments self-destructing by going over the top, a perception of the Conservatives as 'out of touch' might be sharpened if Labour can portray itself as the party of common sense.

(c) More likely still, the Conservatives might fall victim to their own success. Here there are precedents. Once the post-war Labour government had implemented the reforms on which it had been elected, it lost its unique selling point. The Conservatives regained power in 1951, albeit luckily, and retained power through the 1950s. As Attlee ruefully commented after Labour's defeat in 1955, 'today even our opponents cannot put forward something entirely contrary to Labour's view'.

Labour must hope that Mrs Thatcher's success will also change the priorities of the electorate. The more she lays the ghost of the 1970s, the more attention will focus on the new challenges of the 1990s. When governing ceases to be the issue, strong personalities like Mrs Thatcher will be in less demand. When private affluence is taken for granted, the agenda may shift to public squalor. Yet it is difficult for long-lasting governments, and Prime Ministers, to change tack in response to a new agenda – particularly when, as with this administration, the existing image is so sharp. Labour's task is therefore to position itself as the natural party for Britain after Thatcher. Barring the unforeseeable, Labour is most likely to win if, after the next election, Mrs Thatcher, like Mr Attlee, has to acknowledge that she lost the battle because she won the war.

DON'T LOSE IT AGAIN

"Here you are—don't lose it again!"

(Reproduced from our VE-Day issue without apology.)

In 1945, the Conservatives were the party that could not be trusted. In this cartoon from the Mirror, the war-scarred veteran asks voters not to waste peace and victory.

To exploit the opportunities of 1991, in whatever form they come, Labour should show that it has adjusted to change. Although oppositions cannot win elections by themselves they can lose them by failing to adapt. In 1966, the Conservatives failed to learn the lessons of their defeat seventeen months earlier. They were still perceived as tired, out of touch, upper class. They were well beaten. In 1987, Labour had only partly adjusted to political change. Its policies were seen as backward-looking and sectional. It too was thrashed. In 1991, Labour must present the face of the future, not the past. It must convince most voters that it will not waste the gains achieved so painfully under Mrs Thatcher. If it can do so, it should make substantial progress. For when oppositions do capitalise on government weakness they can win support even among voters who remain sceptical about the opposition's own remedies. There were doubts about Churchill in 1951, Wilson in 1964, Heath in 1970 and Thatcher in 1979. Yet in all these cases the government lost.

Chapter 4
Policies

Policies are to parties what engines are to cars: essential to performance but rarely examined in depth by the consumer. A detailed manifesto is essential not because voters read it but because it establishes an image of competence which allows attention to move on to the broader strengths of the party. After twelve years in opposition, the Labour Party must get the policy engine running to show it is 'government ready'.

How can policies be convincing if voters do not understand them or even know what they are? The answer is to persuade the opinion-leaders – the people on whom the voters, aware of their own lack of expertise, must rely. Opinion-leaders fall into two categories: commentators and implementers. Commentators include the broadcasting organisations' specialist correspondents, the heavyweight academics and the columnists from the quality press. Their credibility is based on perceived impartiality (whether they are impartial is irrelevant). Especially when they convey the same basic message, their impact is considerable (Miller *et al.*, 1982). At the next election, Labour needs most of these commentators to say, 'this is the manifesto of a party which is serious about government'.

By contrast, implementers are those charged with carrying out change. They include industrialists, trade unionists and professionals – and more particularly their spokespersons. Their credibility is based not on impartiality but on specialist expertise and functional importance. Any party seeking power cannot afford to have too many implementers going from studio to studio saying, 'this won't work'. In combination, commentators and implementers form a climate of opinion which no serious party, no matter how radical, can afford to disregard.

A striking example of popular reliance on expert opinion comes from televised debates between presidential candidates in the United States. Viewers' initial 'perceptions' of the winner can change over time to fall into line with commentators' judgements. Another American study (Page *et al.*, 1987) examined public opinion on eighty policy areas covered on TV news in the last fifteen years. The findings showed that a single favourable comment from a TV news commentator on a particular policy was associated with four percentage points of opinion change; a favourable report from experts or research studies was worth three points. It seems unlikely that Britain would differ sharply from the American pattern. The message is simple: to influence the public, Labour must first influence those who carry credibility with the public.

Labour's reputation is particularly important in the core areas of defence, law and order, and the economy. After all, the basic tasks of government are to defend the country from attack, maintain law and order, and provide a framework for economic growth. The functions of government can thus be arranged in a pyramid, with these core tasks at its base:

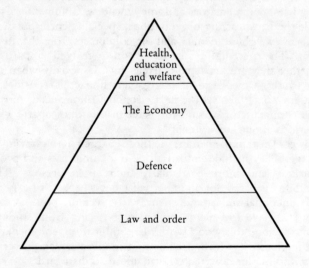

Figure 4.1

Fulfilling these basic tasks is a precondition of achieving 'higher' objectives. For example, the NHS cannot flourish unless the economy is sound. We therefore suspect, though we cannot prove, that any party needs firmness and unity on these basic issues if it is to be seen as fit to govern. Certainly the pyramid seems to fit Labour's current position. The 1987 campaign surely showed that Labour cannot win on the caring issues alone. It must first come close to equalising on more basic issues such as managing the economy. If Labour could catch the Conservatives *before* the next campaign on these 'bottom line' issues, it would be able to win more votes *during* the campaign from its natural and growing lead on the 'higher' issues. Despite Mrs Thatcher, an increasing majority of electors express caring attitudes on many social issues.

The trouble is that the Conservatives dominate the base of the pyramid. Figure 4.2 shows which party has been seen as best at dealing with various issues, averaged across polls taken between 1959 and 1987. The spread looks even but hides a Conservative advantage. The Conservatives dominate the key areas of defence and law and order while Labour is corralled in the welfare segment – health, pensions and education. On the economy, the other core issue, the situation is more complicated. Labour has a declining lead on jobs but the Conservatives are ahead on taxes, prices and, now, strikes. Crucially, the Conservatives have a big lead on the overall question of which party is best for prosperity (see p. 79). In general, the figure demonstrates Labour's need to strengthen its position on the fundamental government tasks of law and order, defence and the economy.

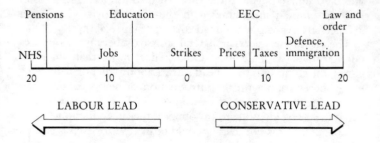

Figure 4.2 Best Party for Specific Issues (average lead 1959–87)

This chapter therefore begins, as will the electorate, at the base of the pyramid with defence, law and order and the economy (including the unions). We then move up the chart and consider health, education and pensions. These six issues have appeared most consistently in the public's list of important national problems during the 1980s. We conclude with a discussion of a newer issue – the environment.

Defence

This section examines the electoral significance of unilateralism. If Labour stays unilateral, this will be the only defence issue which matters. If Labour drops unilateralism, the defence issue is to an extent defused.

Could a unilateralist Labour party win? Unilateralism is and will remain a vote-loser. There is no doubt that a majority of the electorate has always supported Britain's independent nuclear deterrent. Since the early 1950s, the proportion favouring unilateralism has rarely exceeded a third. Every poll has shown more people against unilateralism than for it. The public wants a few cheap nuclear weapons under Britain's control to help deter threats from whatever source – the Soviet Union, the United States, Germany. 'British Gaullism,' says Hugh Berrington (1989), 'sums up the present defence philosophy of the British people.' Whatever happens in international politics, it is most unlikely that this attitude will change. No matter how passionate its commitment, no matter how coherent its arguments, it is not within the power of the Labour Party to convert a majority of voters to unilateralism in the short or medium term. Indeed, as Labour adopted unilateralism in the 1980s, so its ratings on defence, always weak, declined further (Figure 4.3).

The electorate rejects unilateralism partly because it opposes taking 'risks' with defence. On defence, more than on most issues, the status quo has a head start. Labour will normally have more success opposing the introduction of new weapons than supporting the removal of existing ones. Thus it was easier in 1964 for Harold Wilson to oppose the introduction of an independent deterrent than it would be in 1991 for Neil Kinnock to advocate its removal.

No one can be sure how many of the votes Labour has lost on

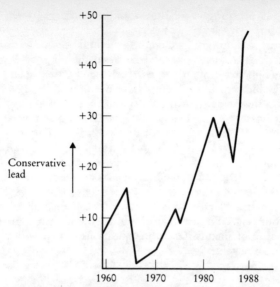

Figure 4.3 Which Is the Best Party on Defence?

defence spring from divisions over the policy rather than the policy itself. When voters are asked to choose from a list of reasons for not voting Labour, 'the dangers of Labour's defence policy' usually runs a few points behind 'Labour's too divided'. None the less, the position of defence near the base of the pyramid means it always has the potential to become a big issue. Given Neil Kinnock is serious about winning the next election outright, a remarkably ambitious objective, he had little choice but to find some international development which justified a switch to multilateralism. He cannot afford to go into the next election, as he did in 1987, with as few as 60 per cent of Labour voters believing Labour has the best defence policy.

A switch of policy would have several electoral advantages. First, the party would become an option for many Conservative and Alliance voters who will not vote for a unilateralist party. Various polls in 1988 showed that between 18 and 31 per cent of non-Labour voters said they would be more likely to vote Labour if it dropped unilateralism, at least twice as many as said 'less likely'.

Secondly, if Labour dropped unilateralism it would be perceived as updating its policies and dissociating itself from extremism.

Thirdly, Labour voters themselves would become less divided on defence. The party has only persuaded about half its voters to support unilateralism. If the party changed policy many of its voters would breathe a sigh of relief and follow suit. (There is no doubting the capacity of the party to influence the views of its own electors even on defence.) We might see a return to the 1960s and 1970s when at most a third of Labour voters advocated unilateralism. Indeed, even in 1988 as many Labour voters (16 per cent) said they would be more likely to vote Labour if it dropped unilateralism as said they would be less likely to do so (14 per cent).

Whether the electoral benefit of a switch to multilateralism would outweigh the cost of an almighty row and exposure to the new charge of inconsistency are questions which will only be answered by events.

Law and Order

Given its position at the base of the pyramid, law and order also has the potential to be electorally significant. In addition, law and order has been growing in explicit importance. By August 1988 law and order came equal second with health on the pollster's chart of national problems, though it had fallen back again slightly by the end of the year. It is an issue of particular concern in London, an area containing many Conservative-held marginals. In the first quarter of 1989, Londoners were nearly twice as likely as people elsewhere to say law and order was an important national problem.

Public opinion on law and order has always been tough but has certainly become no tougher under Mrs Thatcher. If anything it has become more liberal. In this as in other areas the Conservatives have exploited public opinion more than they have influenced it. Thus the slow decline in the size of the majority favouring capital punishment has not been reversed since 1979. And presumably in reaction to the perceived stiffening of sentences, a growing proportion of voters believe we should go easier on people who break the law – up from 27 per cent in 1978 to 44 per cent in 1987.

Law and order is a Conservative issue. Over the past ten years the Conservative lead on this issue (Figure 4.4) has been greater even than on defence. The best that can be said for Labour is (a) that it has recovered slightly from the massive deficits recorded during the Winter of Discontent, and (b) that the Conservative lead slipped in the late 1980s as publicity about crime increased. In 1987, 92 per cent said violent crime had increased over the last few years and there was particular concern about rape (84 per cent said this was an important social problem in 1987, up 17 points on 1979) and drunkenness (63 per cent, up 7). After a dozen years of Mrs Thatcher, the Conservatives can hardly plead for more time for their measures to work.

Law and order is still not fully politicised at present. When pollsters ask which issues are most important in deciding how to vote, law and order drops to sixth or seventh. This reflects some scepticism among the electorate about the ability of any party to do much about crime; in 1987 only 59 per cent said government could do 'quite a bit' to reduce crime. Unless Labour somehow manages to convince most voters it could reduce crime, it may be better off with limited faith in the ability of any government to do so.

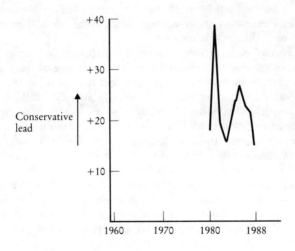

Figure 4.4   Which Is the Best Party on Law and Order?

If law and order does become an issue, Labour's strength is always its concern with the causes of crime. Many people who advocate tough sentences also recognise the social origins of crime. In 1983, 68 per cent agreed that 'if you want to cut crime, cut unemployment'. Labour might benefit from detailed policies on the causes of crime to contrast with the hectoring naivety of Mrs Thatcher.

What Labour does need to do is demonstrate its commitment to order and authority in society. Firmness on law and order will help to secure the base of the electoral pyramid, encouraging the agenda to shift to more favourable social issues. But Labour need not be as adulatory towards the police as Mrs Thatcher. According to Gallup most people recognise the existence of police corruption and favour limits on police power. And doubts are growing about the effectiveness of the police. Between 1981 and 1989 those satisfied with the way their area is policed fell from 75 to 58 per cent. None the less, the police retain more respect than any occupation except doctors. So the proposal in the Policy Review for an independent Police Complaints Authority is likely to be supported by most electors. But many voters are more concerned about the effectiveness of the police. Between 1981 and 1989 those satisfied with the way their area is policed fell from 75 to 58 per cent. The emphasis of the Policy Review on police accountability rather than effectiveness does not address this concern.

Law and order is one of several social issues on which most electors express traditional views. Labour's liberal instincts on social issues such as capital punishment do not mesh well with the values which predominate among its less well-educated working-class supporters. However, with the exception of (Aids-related?) attitudes to homosexuals, 'traditional' values have not become more widespread in the 1980s (Lipsey, Shaw and Willman, 1989). In fact in several areas – divorce, abortion, equality for women and capital punishment – public opinion has become rather more liberal (Rentoul, 1989, pp. 146–51). In any case, attitudes to these issues only influence party allegiance slightly, if at all, suggesting their electoral impact is only latent. Labour's interest is to keep it that way; this may not be possible in a close, rough campaign.

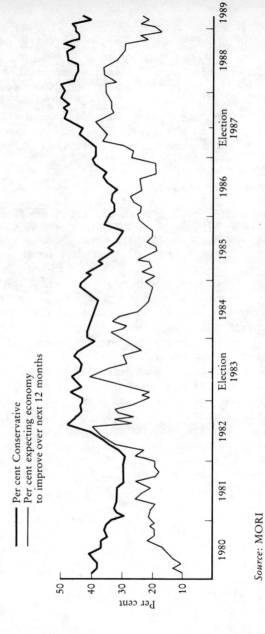

Per cent Conservative

Per cent expecting economy
to improve over next 12 months

Figure 4.5 Economic Optimism and Voting

Source: MORI

The Economy

The economy is always crucial. Figure 4.5 shows how Conservative support in the 1980s moved in tandem with popular expectations about the economy. For example, the Conservative decline in the polls in 1989 owed much to pessimism about the economy. In spring 1989, the electorate was more pessimistic than at any time since 1980. A pre-election boom could easily cause a swing back to the Conservatives. Certainly Labour must assume that in 1991 the Conservatives will synchronise the electoral and economic cycles as skilfully as in 1983 and 1987. This is Labour's biggest single problem.

Managing the Economy

Labour must seek to convince voters it can manage the economy as competently as the Conservatives. This is crucial because credibility on the economy will enhance Labour's appeal among all sections of society. Whatever their social position, most electors see that their own personal well-being is intertwined with the performance of the national economy. Most voters give the same answer to 'which party is best for you personally?' as to 'which party is best for the country?' Labour's task is therefore to appeal to the long-term enlightened interests of voters who recognise how their own prospects depend on the general economic environment.

This means that within the economic sphere Labour has to emphasise production over distribution. If Labour can allay doubts about its ability to produce the goods, its natural lead on sharing them out will come into play. But if those doubts remain, that lead will count for much less. It is not that distribution is irrelevant; most people say economic inequality is increasing, is excessive and should be reduced by government. Eighty per cent or so usually say that the Conservative government's economic policies are 'unfair'. The point is rather that Labour must secure the base of economic competence before 'fair shares' come into play. So the party has no choice but to fight on the battlefield of economic management. To say that Labour should not fight on economic competence because it cannot win on that issue amounts to surrendering before battle is joined.

Labour's ratings on economic management are abysmal. After

Trog's famous comment on the 1959 election. In fact consumer durables are less important than a general atmosphere of prosperity in boosting government popularity.

the 1987 campaign 34 per cent said a Labour government would cause an economic crisis, more than twice the number mentioning the Conservatives (15 per cent) or the Alliance (14 per cent). Questions about which party is best for prosperity have produced equally chilling results:

Table 4.1 'Which Party Would Be Best at Making Britain More Prosperous?' and Comparable Voting Figures, 1979–87

	1979		1983		1987	
	Best for prosperity	Voting figures in same survey	Best for prosperity	Voting figures in same survey	Best for prosperity	Voting figures in same survey
	%	%	%	%	%	%
Conservative	51	46	49	44	52	43
Labour	32	38	20	28	23	32
Liberal/ Alliance	8	14	15	26	12	23
Conservative lead	+19	+8	+29	+16	+29	+11

Source: BBC/Gallup.

Even though Labour probably always does better in the polling booth than on prosperity ratings, Labour's deficit on the economy has been far too big in recent campaigns to sustain a serious bid for power. Little has changed since 1987: in February 1989, the Conservatives led Labour by 45 to 28 per cent on overall management of the economy and more people said a Labour government would not help their living standards than said that it would. Labour was further behind the Conservatives on overall management of the economy than on specific areas such as unemployment, prices, interest rates or even taxation, indicating that the problem is one of general economic credibility. Labour's overall approach is seen as backward-looking as well as ineffective. In 1987, most people believed a Labour government would bring more inflation, strikes, state ownership and union power – that is, a return to the 1970s rather than an advance to the 1990s. In March 1989, the most common opinion was that under Labour prices would go up but unemployment and take-home pay would stay the same.

By contrast, the ratings for the Conservatives reflect Mrs Thatcher's success in convincing half the electorate she has produced structural improvement in the economy. In the 1987 election 53 per cent agreed that 'Britain's economic decline has been halted'. A year later 59 per cent agreed that 'in the long term this government's policies will improve the state of Britain's economy' (even 31 per cent of Labour voters agreed). In March 1989, 52 per cent thought Mrs Thatcher had done a good job 'of managing the economy generally'. Against a twenty-five-year background of relative economic decline, this sense of a recovering economy has undoubtedly been crucial to Conservative success, reinforcing the Conservative's image as the party which enables people to better their own living standards. If there were positive reasons for Mrs Thatcher's election victories in the 1980s, perceived economic revival was prominent among them.

One specific benefit which the Conservatives gained from economic recovery was to recover almost all the ground they had lost on unemployment. By the end of 1988 Labour's lead on unemployment was down to single figures; it is hardly a Labour issue any more. But as unemployment fell so too did public concern about it. Instead inflation edged up the public's chart of urgent problems – and here the massive Conservative lead, established in the mid-1980s, is rapidly decaying.

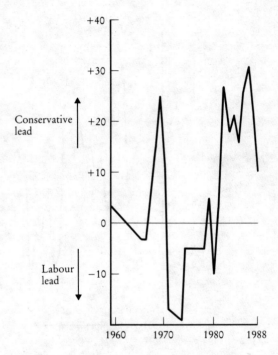

Figure 4.6 Which Is the Best Party on Prices?

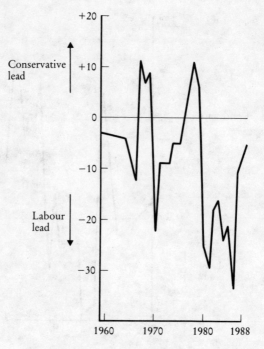

Figure 4.7 Which Is the Best Party on Unemployment?

Projecting economic competence does not mean Labour has to offer tax cuts. Just as Conservative success has been based on general economic revival, not tax cuts, so too will improvements in Labour's ratings on the economy flow from detailed, credible policies on the economy as a whole. Tax is not the issue. In fact even modest tax increases are acceptable. In September 1988, 24 per cent of non-Labour voters said they would be *more* likely to vote Labour as a result of the party's proposals to increase public spending and taxes. Only 20 per cent said these proposals made them less likely to vote Labour. In 1988, most people did not feel they paid too much tax and a growing number advocate tax increases to fund improved public services and benefits:

Table 4.2 Attitudes to Taxes and Public Spending, 1983–7

	1983 %	1984 %	1985 %	1986 %	1987 %
Suppose the government had to choose between these three options. Which should it choose?					
Reduce taxes and spend less on health, education and social benefits	9	6	6	5	3
Keep taxes and spending on these services at the same level as now	54	50	43	44	42
Increase taxes and spend more on health, education and social benefits	32	39	45	46	50

Source: BSA.

Labour's need for general economic credibility does however require the manifesto to be specific on what tax increases will be necessary. There is nothing to be gained, and much to be lost, from fudging the issue.

Regaining Credibility

Clearly Labour has to improve its economic credibility if it is to have any chance of winning the next election. As memories of the 1970s fade, so this task becomes less awesome. By March

1989 as many as 38 per cent said they had no recollection of what things were like when Labour was in power. It is true that those memories which do remain are largely negative: strikes, unions and inflation top the list. But even these images concern the 1970s generally as much as Labour governments specifically. By 1989 more people thought Thatcher (25 per cent) rather than Callaghan (20 per cent) had been in power during the Winter of Discontent – and almost as many said Heath (18 per cent). Clearly, many electors recall a decade rather than a winter of discontent, a period stretching between the miners' strikes of 1974 and 1984 and covering Conservative as well as Labour administrations. So although Thatcher may be seen by many as the leader who 'got us out of the mess', with the passage of time Labour is less often seen as the sole cause of it. This gives at least something on which to build. So how should Labour go about the task of restoring economic credibility? Four elements are:

1. **People**   Economic credibility means Labour demonstrating it has able spokespersons who can talk convincingly about the economy, hold their own in debates with ministers and convey their authority to specialist commentators. Projecting an ability to manage the economy is about competence more than ideology and people as much as policies.

2. **Prudence**   HOW ARE YOU GOING TO PAY FOR IT? is a question which echoes down from past campaigns. Labour is always vulnerable to the charge of a Santa Claus manifesto. As the party now recognises, it must cost its proposals carefully, and, to demonstrate the macroeconomic coherence of its policies, ensure its manifesto can survive the scrutiny of mainstream computer models of the economy.

3. **Don't renationalise, regulate**   Accepting the status of the newly privatised industries will help Labour to be seen as a party which can adapt to change and look forward. Fewer than one in five electors want more state ownership of industry – but equally most now oppose further denationalisation (Table 4.3). Yet in April 1989 57 per cent thought it very or quite likely that a Labour government would 'take away shares of public companies that have been privatised such as British Telecom'. So here is a chance for Labour to seize the middle ground. With the Conservatives committed to further privatisations, Labour can

Table 4.3 State Ownership of Industry

	1983 %	1984 %	1985 %	1986 %	1987 %
Respondent would like					
More	11	10	13	16	16
About the same	33	50	51	49	48
Less	49	36	31	30	30

Source: BSA.

project an image of consolidation by concentrating on measures to improve industrial performance in both the public and the private sectors. The Policy Review's proposals to take *back* British Telecom and the major utilities into public ownership do not project a *forward*-looking image. In general, Labour should regulate rather than renationalise. As Table 4.4 shows, that was the most popular option in 1987 for electricity, steel, telephones and local transport.

Table 4.4 Attitudes to Ownership and Control of Specific Industries, 1987

		Government should	
	Own	*Control prices and profits but not own*	*Neither own nor control*
Electricity	26%	42	23
Steel	26%	40	24
Telephone system	23%	39	29
Local public transport	19%	37	35
Car industry	8%	25	54
Banking and insurance	7%	29	51

Source: BSA.

4. **Supply-side socialism** Labour should continue to examine what its social and public-sector policies can do for the private sector. The growing emphasis within the party on supply-side socialism will allow Labour's strength at the top of the pyramid to leak down towards the base where it is most needed – on ratings for economic competence. For example, collective provision of childcare will not only encourage women to work, it will

also produce a more flexible labour market than if provision is tied to a particular company. As Leadbeater (1987) suggests, Labour must show what its social policies will do for the economy as well as vice versa.

An approach based on pragmatic, managed capitalism would capture the public mood much better than the obsessively non-interventionist stance associated with Mrs Thatcher. We consider three examples here.

(a) *Improving the physical infrastructure*   This is natural Labour territory, made more so by perceptions of Conservative neglect. Labour can surely argue that further progress in the private sector requires strengthening the infrastructure. Take roads, for example. By 1988 55 per cent disapproved of the government's handling of roads and 63 per cent said the Conservatives were not giving value for money on roads. The government's proposals for new roads go some way to meeting these concerns. For Labour, the danger is that the emphasis on public transport in the Policy Review will be seen as irrelevant by the 64 per cent of all households (and the 77 per cent of skilled manual households) which now have access to a car. Recent first-time car buyers want to exercise the flexibility which was the reason for their purchase. They do not want to be stuck in jams but neither do they want to be told to leave the car at home and catch the bus instead. Seventy per cent of car-owners said in February 1989 that an overhaul of public transport would not reduce their use of their car.

(b) *Intervention for innovation*   Most electors remain sympathetic to selective intervention in the private sector. A majority want government to offer financial support for innovation; but only a minority favour government aid to declining industries. New technologies, new factories, new businesses, new products, new jobs – all these are areas where 80 per cent or more believe government should definitely or probably make a financial contribution, even if this might mean an increase in income tax. Labour can argue that the government's ideological refusal to adopt an industrial strategy amounts to an abdication of its responsibility. Labour can suggest further that it alone has the links needed to encourage modernisation in the manufacturing sector. Surprisingly, more people believe manufacturing indus-

THE
CONSERVATIVE MANIFESTO
DOESN'T SAY
ANYTHING ABOUT REDUCING
UNEMPLOYMENT.

IT DOESN'T SAY
ANYTHING ABOUT IMPROVING
THE HEALTH SERVICE.

IT DOESN'T SAY
ANYTHING ABOUT INVESTING
IN EDUCATION.

IT DOESN'T SAY
ANYTHING ABOUT BUILDING
MORE HOUSES.

IT SAYS A LOT
ABOUT THE CONSERVATIVES.

The trouble was, the commentators said just the same about Labour's manifesto in 1987. To achieve credibility in 1991, Labour will need more, and more detailed, policies.

try has considerable influence over Labour than over the Conservatives, who are seen as representatives of finance.

The task for Labour is to identify fresh and effective means of intervention. Few commentators will believe Labour ministers alone are the best judges of where support is needed. The problem of how to intervene, rather than whether to do so, has been a long-running weakness of industrial policy in Britain. In the past Labour has offered few effective solutions, partly because of its commitment to the blunderbuss of nationalisation. Now that commitment has receded, Labour has proposed new mechanisms, such as an investment bank, in the Policy Review. The task now is to convince the commentators that these new institutions will be shielded from short-term politicking and are based on more than spend and hope.

(c) *Improving work skills*   Investment in education and training is traditional Labour territory and equally essential for economic health. Again, however, to convince the commentators and, through them, the voters, Labour will need specific proposals, not general incantations.

In education the public's main priority is to improve skills related to employment. Between 1968 and 1988, the proportion saying British education was satisfactory for career preparation halved from 68 per cent to 32 per cent, a massive decline. Here the Policy Review offers useful proposals – broadening the core curriculum, expanding personal, social and careers education, building on GCSE and developing Records of Achievement.

The Policy Review said little about improving work skills through employee participation. Yet such schemes would strike a responsive chord in public opinion. Most electors believe bad management is a major cause of Britain's economic problems, that poor industrial relations is a key component of bad management, and that industrial relations would be improved by more worker participation. In 1986, for example:

- 80 per cent agreed that industry should share more of its profits with employees;
- 76 per cent said employees with shares in their companies tend to work harder;
- less than a third said managers know best and employees should just go along with their decisions.

And:

- the proportion agreeing that the government should give workers more say in running the places where they work grew from 56 per cent in October 1974 to 68 per cent in 1983.

Here then is another chance for Labour. The party can exploit the long-term trend towards shorter lines of communication, and more employee participation, in firms. But there is a danger Labour's proposals will be seen as a device to increase the power of trade unions. As a growing number of union leaders already recognise, Labour's plans will be more popular if they centre on the employee's direct involvement in the firm and are not routed through trade unions. This will enable Labour to show it has progressed since Callaghan's proposals based on the Bullock Report of the 1970s.

In all these areas, Labour's policy-makers will need flexibility to achieve economic credibility. Traditional sympathies for public transport, declining industries, depressed regions and trade unions will need to be balanced by an increasing emphasis on the private sector, growth points and the individual employee.

Trade Unions

The power of the unions in the workplace and over government is no longer seen as a major problem. Between 1979 and 1987 the proportion saying trade unions have too much power halved from 68 per cent to 31 per cent. In fact there are recent signs of an improvement in the unions' image. In 1988, 68 per cent said that in general 'trade unions are a good thing', one of the highest figures recorded since this question was started in 1954.

For what the unions have received, most voters are truly thankful. The Conservatives benefit from bringing the unions to heel. In 1979, even after the Winter of Discontent, Labour was still ahead as the best party to deal with strikes. By 1988 the Conservatives had captured the issue.

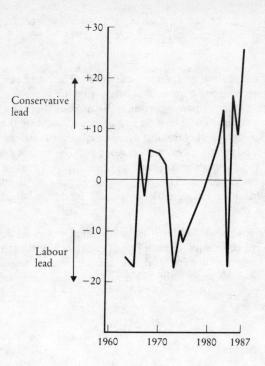

Figure 4.8 Which Is the Best Party on Strikes and Industrial Disputes?

In March 1989, the government's handling of the unions came top of the list when people were asked what were the best things the Conservative government had done.

Can Labour convince the electorate it will not undo the Conservatives' work? Not easily. In April 1989, 63 per cent said it was very or quite likely that a Labour government would remove controls placed on the unions since 1979. Labour would undoubtedly pay some electoral price for proposing to repeal Conservative legislation though it might not be great, particularly if any restoration of collective rights were linked to greater control of union leaders by their members. In 1988, 16 per cent said they would be more likely to vote Labour if it decided not to repeal Conservative trade union laws, compared to 10 per cent saying less likely (the figures for Labour voters were not significantly different). This suggests a relatively small bonus for Labour from accepting Conservative reforms. But the main point is surely that any proposals for repeal would put Labour on the defensive in the next campaign, allowing the Conservatives to claim that Labour is still a reactionary party dominated by the unions.

The way forward is not to repeal laws but to use Labour's special relationship with the unions constructively. Most voters are sympathetic to enhanced union involvement in such traditional issues as health and safety, wages, pensions, working conditions, job protection and equal opportunities. Labour is always rated higher on industrial relations than industrial disputes and there is safety for the party in such detail. Proposals here would not induce the clamour which would emerge over any proposals to repeal Conservative laws.

Another problem is union influence over the Labour Party. But even here the situation is easing. Between 1978 and 1988 the proportion saying the unions have most say in Labour's policies (that is, ahead of the leader, the NEC, the Shadow Cabinet and the PLP) fell from 54 per cent to 35 per cent. Particularly when people are asked to explain in their own words why they do not support Labour, the unions are not prominent. After the 1987 election union influence was only the seventh most common reason given when people were asked why Labour lost. The unions only came eleventh when people were asked to say which issues decided their own vote. When people were asked in September 1987 what Labour would have to do 'for you to vote for them in the next election', only 5 per cent said reduce the power of trade unions in the party compared to 20 per cent mentioning defence and 14 per cent saying get rid of left-wing policies. Other findings, based on direct questioning about Labour's links with the unions, do point to a bigger problem. But overall we feel union influence over the party is an excuse as well as a reason for not voting Labour; and is in any case a declining problem.

Health

Early in 1988, and again in spring 1989, health topped the pollsters' chart of 'the most important issues facing Britain today'. This concern reflects growing dissatisfaction with the NHS. Between 1956 and 1988 the proportion believing 'they are getting a good service from the NHS' fell from 89 per cent to 59 per cent. Between 1983 and 1987 the proportion saying the NHS is well run fell from a half to a third, the biggest decline among fifteen institutions tested. This transformation reflects growing doubts about the hospital service, particularly waiting lists. Ratings of GPs stayed high.

Support for the principle of socialised medicine has not fallen. Most people still support an NHS funded out of taxation and free to all at the point of service. A majority opposes charges for sight tests and dental check-ups, rejects hospital charges for food and accommodation and believes prescription charges are too high (indeed 15 per cent says prescription charges have proved a deterrent against their visiting a doctor). The problem is that a traditional public service is believed to have been harmed by underfunding. Thus health is now well clear at the top of the list for extra government spending, far ahead of pensions and education.

Within the health service the public's main priorities are:

- to reduce waiting lists for operations and consultants' appointments
- to improve staffing levels of hospitals and doctors
- to improve casualty departments
- to improve the condition of hospital buildings

There is little concern about the quality of treatment. It is access to treatment, and the environment in which it is delivered, which is judged unsatisfactory.

The NHS is the jewel in Labour's crown. Over the past quarter century the party's lead on the NHS has on average been even larger than its deficit on defence. Conversely, the NHS is the Conservatives' great weakness. In November 1988, eight out of ten disapproved of the government's handling of the health service. The government's review proposals have caused additional problems for the Conservatives. In February 1989, 71 per cent of those who had heard of these proposals disapproved of them and most thought their real purpose was to lead to privatisation of the NHS. Most people anticipated that the NHS would be in worse shape ten years hence, a telling indictment of the Conservatives' handling of it.

Figure 4.9   Which Is the Best Party on Health?

As with other issues there is a danger to the party in presenting health policy in terms of public/private divisions. Support for the NHS does not mean opposition to private medicine. In fact private medicine is widely seen as a sector which should be separate from the NHS and towards which government should be neutral. Thus most electors oppose tax breaks for people (including the over 60s) taking out private health insurance but just one in ten – and only one in five Labour voters – believe private medical treatment should be abolished. Most voters share neither Conservative support nor Labour opposition to private provision; electors are uninterested in ideological battle-grounds. Their concern is the availability and quality of care on the NHS.

Labour won the battle to be seen as the best party for health

UNDER THE TORIES YOUR CHILD'S EDUCATION COULD DEPEND ON JUST ONE BOOK.

YOUR CHEQUE BOOK.

**The Tories plan to let State schools charge fees if they want to.
If you don't want to pay, don't vote Tory.**

THE COUNTRY'S CRYING OUT FOR CHANGE. VOTE LABOUR

Labour's advertising was more confident in 1987 but Labour cannot win on social issues alone.

on the day the NHS started. Labour's task now is not to extend its lead but is to improve its ratings on the key issues of defence, law and order and the economy. This will enable Labour's natural lead on health to pull its electoral weight.

Education

Education is a steady second-division issue. In 1988, it typically ranked eighth in the list of most important issues facing the country; fourth in a precoded list of issues which are personally important in shaping votes; and second (a long way behind health) as a priority for extra government spending.

Education is a neat cameo of Thatcherism's general themes. First, the public's perception of decline provides the underlying agenda. Between 1963 and 1986, the proportion satisfied with 'the education children are getting today' halved. Secondly, there is considerable sympathy for measures taken by government to reverse decline. In 1987, 65 per cent of parents with children at state secondary schools supported the national curriculum and 71 per cent supported national testing (however, opting-out is unpopular). Thirdly, the Conservatives receive some reward for their measures – or at least for their impression of activity. By 1988 the Conservatives had caught up with Labour as 'the party most likely to improve standards of education' (see Figure 4.10). Finally, Labour is left wondering how to get the ball back from a hard-running government.

Fighting the old war against private education is not the way forward. As with private health, most voters are neither concerned about nor opposed to private schools. In 1987, only 11 per cent of the electorate (and 20 per cent of Labour identifiers) said there should be no private schools at all. Indeed half of those with children at state secondary schools say they would send their children to private schools if they could afford it.

Nor is there any mileage in opposing the remaining grammar schools. Most polls show more parents would prefer a selective system to a comprehensive one, albeit with selection based on continuous assessment rather than the old 11 + exam.

The priority must surely be to use education as a display case for supply-side socialism. If Labour can convince voters it has specific proposals for education which will bring more flexible

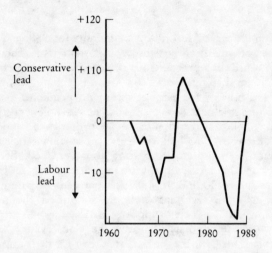

Figure 4.10 Which Is the Best Party on Education?

and better-prepared people into the workforce, that will enable Labour's traditional strength on education to transfer to the more crucial area of economic competence.

Secondary education should be a main thrust of these new proposals. A growing proportion of electors believe secondary schools should be the first recipient of any extra resources for education. Parents are particularly keen to see:

● firmer discipline
● more and better teachers
● more encouragement of competitive sports
● improved provision of textbooks
● more attention to science and maths
● improved careers education

Pensions and Personal Wealth

Pensions are at the bottom of the second division of issues. They barely register when people are asked about the single most important problem facing Britain but usually struggle up to seventh or eighth when people are asked to name two such problems. None the less, in the main pensions are still provided collectively and the issue can be used to reinforce the uncaring image of the Conservatives among young and old alike.

The more important pensions become, the more Labour will benefit. Labour has always led on pensions as Figure 4.11 shows.

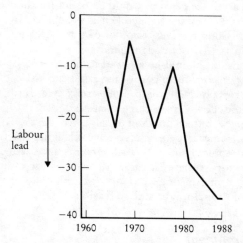

Figure 4.11   Which Is the Best Party on Pensions?

This lead at least matches Labour's strength on the NHS. Under Mrs Thatcher's government, the Conservatives have lost further ground. Between 1979 and 1988, the proportion of the whole electorate saying pensions and retirement pay give value for money fell from 43 per cent to 25 per cent. In 1988, 62 per cent thought pensioners were worse off than in 1979 and 76 per cent disapproved of how the government was handling pensions. Whatever the government does to the state pension, Labour will still be the preferred party in 1991.

When people are asked to choose their first priority for extra cash benefits, pensions consistently come top, ahead of extra support for the disabled, the unemployed and child benefits.

The Policy Review proposal on pensions will surely help Labour to gain, or at least maintain, support. Who can object to a substantial increase in the basic pension or to a bonus for the over 75s? More important, Labour's objective of making the period from 60 to 70 a decade of flexibility for men and women will also be attractive if it can be achieved within the fundamental constraint of projecting financial prudence.

Again Labour needs to watch out for the public/private trap. Limiting private pension schemes would portray the party as regulating against quality. In 1987, a majority of voters for each party said a private pension would be better for them personally than the State Earnings Related Pensions Scheme. In 1986, three out of four Conservatives, two out of three Alliance supporters and one in two Labour identifiers said people who can afford private pensions should be allowed to buy them.

Private pensions form part of the rapid expansion of personal wealth in Britain. Pay now provides only two-thirds of household income, down from three quarters ten years ago. By the year 2000 the return on capital may provide a quarter of all personal income as people invest wealth inherited from first-generation home-owners. In such circumstances Labour might pay an electoral price if it discriminated against capital and in favour of earned income; though discriminating against large amounts of capital might still be feasible.

The Environment

In May 1989, pollution and the environment reached sixth place in the public's list of important national problems. It remains to be seen whether the issue has staying power but certainly public concern about the environment has increased during the 1980s. In November 1988, about half of Gallup's sample claimed to be 'greatly concerned or worried' about such issues as nuclear waste, depletion of forests and the greenhouse effect. In every case, anxieties had grown since 1982 (concern about pollution 'where you live' was much less and had only increased substantially about water quality).

More significantly, the proportion saying they wanted environmental protection to take priority over economic growth had also risen – from 49 per cent in 1982 to 70 per cent in 1988. Woebetide any major party which takes this finding literally but clearly all parties must now aim to combine environmental protection and economic growth.

The issue is still up for grabs. Gallup found that 36 per cent either did not know which party came closest to their views on the environment or said no party came close. Labour, the Conservatives and the Greens were level, each rated best by between 17 and 19 per cent. Labour surely has room to improve here even though it seems unlikely either major party will capture the issue.

If Labour can overcome its smoke-stack, producer image, there are some chances on this issue. This is an area where the vast majority of voters recognise the need for government intervention. In November 1988, 88 per cent thought that government should legislate to control pollution; only 5 per cent favoured self-regulation. Equally, current government policy is believed to favour industry, at least in agriculture. In March 1988, 77 per cent agreed that the government was doing too much to protect the food industry and not enough to protect consumers. The proposals in the Policy Review to curb pollution fit in well with a strategy of regulating, rather than running, industry. As with other issues, Labour has an opportunity to progress but its overall need for credibility as a potential government means the proposals must be practical.

Conclusion

Chapter 5
A Strategy for Labour

The evidence we have reviewed confirms that it will require a major transformation of the political landscape for Labour to win a majority in 1991. Labour needs a swing of 8 per cent but since 1945 the largest swing has been 5 per cent (in 1979); and the largest swing to Labour a mere 3 per cent (Crewe, 1989). To stand any real chance, Labour will have to perform brilliantly and benefit from factors beyond its control, such as incompetence by the government and an economic recession. In other words, Labour cannot ensure victory through its own efforts: it can only act to raise (or lower) the odds of success.

To give itself the best possible chance Labour does not need fancy strategies based on targeting particular social groups or types of seat (except for the obvious tactic of concentrating on the marginals). Indeed, seemingly sophisticated targeting may actually be counterproductive because appeals to sectional interest groups could well put off more of those outside the groups than it attracts within them. Instead, Labour should appeal across nearly all social groups with a general approach which aims to convince many, many more people that the party is 'fit to govern'. This means demonstrating that the party is united, the policy programme is credible and the leadership is competent. This is no easy task. Producing a policy programme which seems credible to a majority of the people and commands the support of an overwhelming majority in the party would be no mean feat. Within the overall programme the crucial areas are the economy and defence. The party's commitment on the caring issues is widely accepted, but this simply has to be accompanied by much more confidence in Labour's plans to deliver prosperity and security. Labour will be greatly helped if a good number of the less partisan expert commentators speak favourably of the viability of Labour's programme.

Yet even if ratings on unity and policy improve, Labour is still faced with the problem that as long as it is out of office the party can only suggest that it would govern competently. It cannot prove its ability. *It is Catch 22 – Labour needs to improve its credibility in order to receive enough votes to win outright, but can only improve credibility sufficiently by a period of competent government.*

All this does not mean, though, that Labour is consigned to perpetual opposition. There is a significant chance of the next election resulting in a hung Parliament. Indeed David Butler suggested in 1986 that long-term trends meant the odds of any general election producing a hung Parliament were at least even. In view of the poor performance of the opposition parties in 1987, and to some extent since then, this now seems to exaggerate the odds. But even if the chances of a hung Parliament are only one in three, there is still a 70 per cent probability that at least one of the next three elections will produce this outcome. A hung Parliament may offer Labour the opportunity to show that it is fit to govern through its performance in a minority or coalition government. This might improve the party's general reputation sufficiently for it to win a later election outright.

However, suppose Labour does get back into sole power by this route. Would this secure Labour's real objective of reshaping society? Would one or even two Labour governments be able to produce permanent change? As long as Conservative governments largely conserved the status quo rather than reversed progress, developments under Labour governments had long-term value. Achievements were limited, but at least they stuck. Obviously, the Thatcher government has destroyed this process. As long as the Conservative leadership stays in the hands of the right, to make net progress Labour will need to govern not just some of the time but most of it. (If the Conservative leadership shifts towards the centre and acts competently, Labour's chances of any power at all could be even more limited.) Yet since the war Labour has managed to win a reasonable working majority only twice while the Conservatives have done so seven times. Labour will do very well to catch the Conservatives in the near future. The idea that Labour could rapidly replace the Conservatives as the dominant party stretches the imagination.

The obvious alternative to an 'all or, usually, nothing approach' is for Labour to make a clear commitment to democracy and justice and embrace electoral reform. There is, of course, a strong case in principle for everyone being entitled to a vote of similar worth. And even in practice the price of Labour's adherence to the current voting system has been high. As the Labour Campaign for Electoral Reform argues:

> with a more representative electoral system there would have been – no Poll Tax; no Trident; no abolition of the GLC, ILEA and the Metropolitan authorities; no opting out for schools; no halt to council house building; no budget for the rich. There would be protection for the NHS and the welfare state and a fair deal for Trade Unions. Furthermore, effective sanctions would have been imposed on South Africa long ago. The people who depend on Labour are not well served by Labour's adherence to an electoral system which is costing them dearly.

Furthermore, supporting a change in the voting system may now be in Labour's own interest. Labour is not significantly overrepresented at present – it has 35 per cent of the seats from 31 per cent of the UK vote. It is the Conservatives who are treated overgenerously – with 58 per cent of the seats from 42 per cent of the vote. If Labour cannot win regular majorities, what is the point in supporting a system which puts the Conservatives in power time and time again? The cost to Labour of a fair voting system would be the ending of the slim chance of majority rule based on a clear minority of votes. The obvious benefit is that the Conservatives could not rule on this basis either.

But there are several other advantages which are specific to Labour. First, Labour could give its own reputation a boost if it adopted electoral reform before the next election. In changing policy Labour could claim to be acting in the general interest. In particular, Labour could argue that PR would help to reunite the country by greatly reducing the regional imbalances in where parties win seats. (And Labour would gain fair representation in the South upon which to build in the long term.) Adopting electoral reform would mean that the party would no longer be arguing for a more equal distribution of income and wealth and against a fairer distribution of another source of power – seats in the Commons. However, the longer Labour delays, the more likely it is that the party's eventual acceptance of 'one vote of one value' will be seen as either bowing to the inevitable or just changing policy when it suits. Secondly, a move to reform would isolate the Conservatives, exposing them again as a reactionary party opposed to fairness. Thirdly, support for reform would cut some of the distinct ground from beneath the SLD and thus increase Labour's appeal among 1987 Alliance voters. Fourthly, it would enhance Labour's prospects of power through a coalition by showing that the left and centre, but not the right, shared a commitment to a decent democracy. Fifthly, it could weaken Conservative support among non-Thatcherite voters who, for whatever reason, fear a majority Labour government. The Conservatives would struggle in their efforts to win support on the basis of stopping Labour. Sixthly, the realistic prospect of a share in power might help activists to appreciate the pay-off from unity. Seventhly, the need to be prepared for a hung Parliament would be more transparent. There would be time for proper consultation on Labour's strategy, consultation which could give a voice for the members, and a mandate for the leadership, in post-election negotiations.

Labour should not have great difficulty persuading most of its voters to go along with electoral reform. For the 1987 Harris/ITN exit poll showed that Labour voters were equally divided on whether the present system should be retained or changed to a form of proportional representation. This, of course, was despite the stated opposition of the party. A switch of policy would itself bring many more Labour voters round to support for electoral reform.

A common objection to electoral reform is that coalition government would be an inevitable result. This is so if no party ever gets near to majority support. But the 'if' is important – in the very long term Labour must hope to govern alone with majority support. But in the medium term coalitions as such would not impede progress towards Labour's goals. The necessity of coalition might stop Labour carrying through certain radical policies – but only because Labour lacked majority support for its programme. Those committed to democracy should not find this too much of an obstacle! If Labour approached coalitions positively – willing to make some compromises but determined to assert its rights as senior partner – its popular objectives could be achieved, while the party tried to build support for unpopular policies to which it remained committed. Certainly coalitions would enable Labour to achieve

This question from 1970 will be just as valid in 1991. Labour does not need new ideals, it needs new belief in its ability to govern.

considerably more than if it remains in the role of Her Majesty's Loyal Opposition.

It is not surprising that polls show more people against coalition government than in favour. For example, respondents in the 1987 BSA survey were asked, 'Which do you think is generally better for Britain ... to have a government formed by one political party or for two or more parties to get together to form a government?' Fifty-eight per cent favoured the first option; 37 per cent the second. But this does not imply that the coalition consequence of electoral reform would be unpopular. For the survey question, quite reasonably, is a question about the issue in general, not about whether there ought to be a coalition when all parties have minority support. In view of this, the level of support for a coalition is surprisingly high. We have not come across a poll which asked something like – 'If no party gets a majority of the votes, should the party with most votes be able to form a majority government OR should two or more parties get together to form a government?' But the evidence in

Table 5.1 Views of Labour and SLD Voters on a Pact for a Coalition

Q.   If at the next general election Labour were to have a pact with the new Social and Liberal Democratic Party so that if they won enough seats they would support each other in forming a new government, would that make you more or less likely to vote Labour or would it make no difference?

	Vote intention 1988	
	Lab (N=348) %	SLD (N=135) %
More likely	25	38
Less likely	13	19
No difference	59	35
Don't know/no answer	3	9

Source: NOP/Panorama, February 1988.

(Note that we do not know how many Democrats who opposed the pact would abstain or vote for other parties; nor whether such a pact would attract any Conservative voters. So it is uncertain how overall party support would be affected, but it appears that Labour stands to gain.)

Table 5.1 about a possible coalition between Labour and the SLD suggests that this prospect might benefit Labour.

We will not discuss here the whole range of options for electoral reform. Support for the principle has to strengthen before specifics become important. However, one possibility that has attracted attention is the Alternative Vote (AV). Under AV single member constituencies remain, so preserving the link between the elector and a single representative in Parliament. (This is valued by many though we cannot see how this is preferable to multimember constituencies which enable many more people to go to an MP of their preferred party.) Under AV, instead of marking a single cross, voters number the candidates in order of preference. If no candidate receives a majority of first preferences, the bottom one is eliminated and her or his supporters have their votes transferred to their next preference. This process continues until one candidate obtains a majority of votes.

There has always been some sympathy for AV in the Labour Party. It was this system which a Labour government sought to introduce in 1931. The bill passed through the Commons, only to be wrecked by the Lords. AV is a one-ballot version of the exhaustive ballot used in Labour Party leadership elections. One appeal of AV for Labour is that it would redistribute more seats from the Conservatives to the centre party(ies) than from Labour to the centre. This is because the Alliance finished second in most Conservative seats, but not most Labour seats. Therefore, assuming that Conservative and Labour voters would transfer mainly to the centre party(ies), more Conservatives would be vulnerable to being overtaken by centre party candidates.

Table 5.2 gives the number of seats each party might have won had AV been in operation in 1987. This does show the Conservatives losing more than twice as many seats as Labour. However, the main point is that the Conservatives would still have obtained a clear majority. (Even if Labour had received 60 per cent of the transferred votes where it competed for first place in Conservative marginals, the Conservatives would still have gained some 333 seats and remained in power.) AV, therefore, fails to pass the test of fair representation. It would only slightly reduce the inequality in the system and, thus, the ability of a party to win a majority of seats from a minority of votes. Instead

Table 5.2 Comparison of Simulated AV 'Result' in 1987 with
Actual Outcome

	Seats in the Commons		
	AV	Actual	Change
Conservative	351	376	−25
Labour	218	229	−11
Alliance	53	22	+31
Nationalist	11	6	+ 5

Assumptions underlying AV simulation:

1. All first preferences would be as the votes were cast in 1987.
2. Votes transferred from the Alliance, the Nationalists and other minor parties would divide equally between the two biggest parties.
3. Where votes are transferred from the Conservatives or Labour, 80 per cent would go to the Alliance/Nationalist and the remaining 20 per cent would go to the other major party.

of the three or four point lead the two major parties currently need for a majority, with AV they would probably need a lead in the range of six to eight points, certainly out of Labour's reach. This does not represent sufficient reform.

We believe, therefore, that Labour should support a proportional or nearly proportional system. The party would then have to debate the merits of different systems and consider a strategy to bring about reform. After all, any hope of changing the voting system depends on the Conservatives first being defeated under the current rules. Once Labour is committed to electoral reform there is a reasonable argument for an electoral pact with the SLD (and indeed other minor parties which might hope to gain from PR) to make this task easier. Any proposals for a pact based simply on opposition to the Thatcher government would smack too much of desperate self-interest. But if both Labour and the SLD were committed to fair representation the pact could be justified as a means to this end. One possibility would be a pact built around a joint commitment to a referendum on electoral reform. Certainly, Labour should not assume the centre vote will be insignificant in 1991.

There are, quite reasonably, reservations within the party about pacts. After all, standing down candidates would deny some Labour supporters the opportunity to vote for the party. But against this feeling must be weighed the potential benefits of both defeating this government and introducing a system in which the number of 'wasted' votes is far less. Many supporters in places where voting Labour never contributes to Labour victories would find that they had an effective vote in a fairer system.

A pact based on electoral reform would have a far greater chance of success than one lacking this clear objective. There would be a major incentive for SLD supporters to switch to Labour rather than the Conservatives. (While, in all likelihood, the Democrats would still pick up more Labour *votes* than vice versa, this does not mean that they would gain more *seats*. For Labour starts, on average, with a smaller deficit in the Conservative seats it might hope to win.) In addition, the chance of electoral reform should deter damaging interventions from smaller parties which do not formally join the pact. Even in the absence of a joint commitment to electoral reform, support for a pact is surprisingly high. A MORI poll soon after the 1987 election showed nearly half of Labour voters and 40 per cent of 'Alliance' voters in favour of the parties 'agreeing to put up a single candidate in each constituency to oppose the Conservative candidate'. This may not be a sensible or practical option, but support for it was not merely due to post-election 'blues'. As Table 5.3 shows, by early 1988 this option was clearly the more popular among Labour voters.

Table 5.3 One Candidate in Each Seat? Preferences of Those Likely or Inclined to Vote Labour or SLD

	Labour %	SLD %
Both parties fight every seat	36	36
Only one fight each seat	53	44
Don't know/no answer	11	20

Source: NOP/Panorama, February 1988.

We shall not go further into the psephological details of pacts and PR. We must conclude by returning to Labour's present stance on the issue. Labour's opposition to reform is wrong not just because the party's principles demand support for 'one person, one vote, one worth'. Labour's policy represents a failure to even search for all democratic means of attempting to stop the programmes of the Thatcher governments. Labour has not sought to challenge the right to rule of a government elected by a minority of votes, presumably because of some desperate notion that soon 'the pendulum will swing' to Labour. In upholding the voting system the party closes its mind to democratic options for more effective opposition, so making the prospects of Conservative victories greater. Labour is left with neither power nor a principled position on the voting system. Many of those who have borne the heaviest burden of Thatcher's policies are left with little hope that there will be a change of government. So why, oh why, does Labour still support a system which continues to turn a minority vote for the Conservatives into massive power for a right-wing government?

Appendix
The Labour Party and Social Change

This appendix discusses many characteristics of the social structure in Britain, with emphasis on trends into the 1990s and their electoral implications. We begin with a table which summarises the main social changes and their impact on Labour. Sections on the individual characteristics follow, after which those most important to voting are brought together to provide a more detailed picture of the electorate.

The summary table makes it plain that social change has worked against Labour. However, the 'expected' loss of votes is not as large as Table A.1 perhaps suggests. Many of the changes overlap and so cannot be added together as though they were separate effects. Although there is insufficient data to estimate reliably Labour's total expected loss of votes due to changes in the social structure, we 'guesstimate' that the likely loss between 1964 and 1987 was in the range from six to eight percentage points. This is certainly less than the actual loss of 13.3 points. Yet even this expected loss was not an inevitable one. Labour was not, is not, and will not be a helpless victim of social change. A political party has opportunities to adapt – to change with society – to give itself a fair chance of at least hanging on to its share of the vote. Thus in this chapter we cover a wide range of social characteristics not merely to show their likely impact on Labour, but more importantly to describe the society which Labour must prove itself fit to govern.

Table A.1 Social Change in Britain

Characteristic	Change	Impact on Labour (with relative size)
WORK-BASED CHANGES		
Class	Working-class only about three-quarters the size it was 25 years ago. Now down to about 40%, with salariat approaching 30% and still growing.	Unfavourable (Large)
Industry sector	Manufacturing employed 34% in 1971, just 22% in 1987. 19% projected for 1995, when service sector will employ a massive 70%.	Unfavourable (Small)
Production sector	Long-term growth in public sector reversed in 1980s. Employment in public corporations halved to 4%, 1981–7, but employment in public services stable over this period and not projected to decline. Three-quarters of those in jobs work in private sector.	Unfavourable (Small)
Self-employment	After long stability at around 8% of those in work, sizable increase in 1980s to 11.5% in 1987. Projected to be 12.7% of total employment by 1995.	Unfavourable (Small)
Size of firm	In manufacturing, the proportion working in units of 500+ employees fell from a half to a third, 1972–87. This trend may slow as manufacturing recovers.	Unfavourable (Small)
Union membership	Fell from 51% of the workforce in 1979 to just 37% in 1986, a loss of nearly 3 million members. But now bottoming out.	Unfavourable (Small)
State dependency	Between 1979 and 1986, numbers receiving supplementary benefit increased from 3.0 to 4.9 million. Numbers unlikely to increase at this rate in the 1990s.	Favourable (Small)

Characteristic	Change	Impact on Labour (with relative size)
OTHER SOCIAL CHANGES		
Housing	Owner-occupied homes were 50% of dwellings in 1971, 55% in 1981 and 65% in 1988. Still rising though plateau must eventually be reached.	Unfavourable (Medium)
Shares	Ownership up from about 6% in 1979 to 18–20% in early 1987. Building society flotations could increase this further.	Unfavourable (Very small)
Gender	In 1987, 43% of those in work were women, up from 38% in 1975, with slight further rise to 44% in 1995 projected.	Favourable (Very small)
Age	15–29s down from 29% in 1985 to 28% in 1991 and 23% in 2001. Pensionable age group about 23% until 2001, then up to 26% by 2021.	Unfavourable (Very small)
Ethnic minorities	4.5% of population in 1986 and increasing a little – by 90,000 a year. Expected to stabilise at about 7 per cent eventually.	Favourable (Very small)
Education	Proportion with a degree should roughly double to 15% – but this could take half a century!	Favourable (Very small)
Parental influences	Proportion with working-class father down only a tenth since 1964. Those claiming Labour mother up from 21% in 1964 to 42% in 1983 (only 27% claimed Conservative mother), though no further growth projected in recall of Labour parents.	Favourable (Small to medium)

Work-based Social Change

Social Class

Putting a figure on the size of the working class in the late 1980s greatly depends on how it is defined. In a Marxist sense, the vast majority of people remain in the working class as they are only able to earn a living by selling their labour. However, this is not the position if one looks at the traditional class divide of manual versus non-manual work. Nowadays, only just under half of those in employment are manual workers. In 1951, the proportion was seven in ten. Despite this, market research 'social grade' classifications suggest that the combined size of the C2, D and E 'working-class' groups is still as high as 60 per cent of the electorate. (C2 = skilled manual workers; D = semi- and unskilled manual workers; E = those dependent on state benefits.) But we disagree with the way this scheme defines the working class, as well as the 'Head of household' classification procedure.

Instead, we turn to the 'Goldthorpe' scheme for a class measure more solidly founded on economic interests. This scheme excludes the self-employed, along with foremen and technicians, from the working class. Thus the working class is defined more accurately in terms of the section of society to which Labour has traditionally appealed. When married, working women are classified according to their jobs and not their husbands', the size of the 'Goldthorpe' working class comes to a little under 40 per cent of the population (see Table A.2). Even if the manual foremen are included and married women are given a class on the basis of their husbands' jobs, the working class is still not more than half of the electorate.

Although the current Goldthorpe figures do not have precise equivalents before 1983, we estimate that the working class is now a quarter smaller than it was twenty-five years ago (a fall of around thirteen percentage points). Other measures, too, show a reduction in the range from a fifth to approaching a third. In contrast, the salariat – professionals and managers – has expanded by over a half (about ten points) and the routine non-manual class by about a third. The salariat has expanded unevenly, though, with professionals accounting for an increasingly high proportion of it. By 1995, they will outnumber

Table A.2 Party by Social Class, 1987

	Salariat	Routine non-manual	Petty-bourgeoisie	Manual foremen, technicians	Working class
Percentage of sample (%)	28	18	10	5	39
	%	%	%	%	%
Conservative	54	49	62	47	30
Labour	20	25	21	28	50
Alliance	25	25	15	23	19

Source: BSA (1987).

managers by roughly fifteen to eight (this and many of the forecasts in this chapter are from Institute for Employment Research, 1988). In 1971, this ratio was ten to eight. Professionals are somewhat less Conservative than managers.

If recent trends continue, class structure changes in the near future will be less rapid than in the late 1970s and early 1980s. By the mid-1990s, the salariat should amount to 30 per cent and the petty-bourgeoisie 11–12 per cent. These changes will be offset in the main by further shrinking of the working class, down to 36 per cent or so. This shrinkage will be concentrated on unskilled (pro-Labour) jobs.

These changes are very important, since class and party are still related (Table A.2). If, since 1964, only class sizes had changed, not the voting patterns within them, then Labour's vote would have dropped by about eight percentage points (the actual fall was 13.3 points). Whereas Labour could be assured of victory in the 1960s if it picked up 70 per cent of the working-class vote, nowadays even a recovery to this position in the working class would not result in victory without gains among other classes. Thus a strategy which concentrates upon greatly improving the Labour vote within its traditional social base would have to be miraculously successful to prove sufficient. Labour has lost votes fairly evenly across different classes and any recovery is most likely to be based on increased support from all classes.

Industry Sector

The dramatic decline in employment in manufacturing industry is illustrated in Table A.3. Only about a sixth of the sharp decline in manufacturing employment in the early 1980s can be explained by firms contracting out services previously performed in house, without significant changes in the jobs themselves (MSC Labour Market Report, June 1987). The bulk of the drop was 'real'. Even though the rate of decline in manufacturing employment has slowed, by the mid-1990s less than a fifth of those employed will be working in manufacturing.

Within the service sector, business and miscellaneous services will continue to be the biggest growth area. Among 'business' services are banking, insurance, property dealing, legal services, accounting, technical services, advertising, leasing, and various

Table A.3 Distribution of Total Employment by Industry Sector, 1954–95

	1954 %	1971 %	1981 %	1987 %	Projection 1995 %
Primary sector:					
Agriculture	5.3	3.0	2.5	2.2	1.9
Utilities, mining etc.	5.3	3.2	3.0	2.0	1.6
Construction	6.1	6.4	6.3	6.3	6.6
Manufacturing	34.7	33.5	26.2	21.5	19.2
Service sector:					
Distribution, transport and communication	24.7	24.6	26.4	27.1	27.0
Business and miscellaneous services	9.1	11.7	15.4	20.2	23.5
Health, education and public administration	14.8	17.5	20.3	20.7	20.1

Source: IER (1988).

consultancies. 'Miscellaneous' services include cleaning, social and community work, broadcasting, the arts, sports and other recreation, and various services such as unions and churches. Both parts of this expanding sector have grown greatly and in the 1990s will employ over twice the number they did in 1971.

Health and education now account for some 12 per cent of total employment. This is more than twice the 1954 figure of 5.4 per cent. However, the upward trend has been halted. Meanwhile, the proportion working in public administration has fallen only slightly, from 9.5 per cent in 1954 to 8.7 per cent in 1987. A fall to below 8 per cent is projected for 1995, but this estimate is presumably more sensitive to political developments than figures for other sectors.

Within all industrial sectors the proportion of manual workers has declined and will continue to do so. In 1987, only 61 per cent of those in manufacturing were either craft or skilled manual workers, operatives or labourers (in 1971 – 70 per cent; by 1995 – 59 per cent). In other words, this group of manufacturing workers – a rough and ready measure of those people who are paid to make things – now amounts to only about one in eight of those in employment.

Naturally, support for Labour is highest in the manufacturing sector, but the differences are perhaps less than expected and much less than class differences.

Table A.4 Party by Industry Sector, 1987

	Manu-facturing	Distri-bution, transport etc	Business and miscel-laneous services	Health, education and public adminis-tration
	%	%	%	%
Conservative	42	54	53	36
Labour	37	28	25	33
Alliance	20	17	20	29

Source: BSA (1987).

On the basis of the figures in Tables A.3 and A.4 the expected cost to Labour of industry sector changes has been small – a loss of just 1 to 2 per cent since 1971. The shift to services will not help Labour, but neither is it a major handicap. Of course, in a broader sense it is important that Labour's programme takes proper account of the extent to which the service sector dominates employment in Britain.

Production Sector

The long-term growth in public sector employment has been halted and reversed in the 1980s, down from 30 per cent in 1981 to 26 per cent in 1987. This is due entirely to a cut of one-half in numbers working in public *corporations*. Government and public *services* provided 22 per cent of jobs in both 1981 and 1987. By 1991 only a tiny percentage will be working in public corporations and the private sector will account, in all likelihood, for over three-quarters of employment, just as it did thirty years ago.

As Table A.5 shows, both Labour and the centre parties do better among public sector employees. Indeed, comparing within classes, Labour support is ten or more points higher among the 'public sector salariat' than among equivalent people

Table A.5 Party by Production Sector, 1987

	Private sector %	Public corporations %	Government/ public services %
Conservative	51	33	32
Labour	30	42	36
Alliance	18	23	30

Source: BSA (1987).

in the private sector. Within the working class, Labour does about fifteen points better among those employed in public corporations than among equivalent workers in the private sector.

The instant change of ownership produced by privatisation does not imply a sudden electoral impact. But in the long term Labour will lose an advantage of a little less than 1 per cent of the total vote if the voting pattern of workers in the former public corporations comes to resemble that of the rest of the working class.

Self-employment

After a long period of stability, self-employment has risen sharply in the 1980s (Table A.6). By 1988, some 2.98 million people in the UK were self-employed. While the rate of increase will slow down in the future, as fewer people are made redundant than during the recession, the self-employed are likely to number about 3.4 million by the mid-1990s.

Table A.6 Self-employed: Percentage of Total Employment

				Projections	
1954	1975	1981	1987	1992	1995
8.1	8.0	8.7	11.5	12.3	12.7

Source: IER (1988).

Not surprisingly, support for Labour among the self-employed is limited – generally under one-fifth. Thus the increase in self-employment is likely to count against Labour. On the basis that Labour support is twenty percentage points lower among the self-employed than among employees, and that 60 per cent of the electorate is in work, the increase in self-employment between 1979 and 1987 would have cost Labour four-tenths of 1 per cent of the total vote. The Conservatives' expected gain is a little higher, as they do better among the self-employed at the expense of all other parties. This apparently small electoral impact could be magnified by an influence of self-employment on the families of those directly concerned. On the other hand, Conservative voters may be more likely to go into self-employment in the first place; certainly the biggest expansion in self-employment has been in the Conservative regions of the South of England, especially the South-West and East Anglia. Overall, the expansion of self-employment may be reinforcing Conservative votes but it will not cause a major depletion in Labour's support.

Size of Firm

Declining employment in large manufacturing plants will also work against Labour with its traditional strength in large, unionised factories. Within the manufacturing sector, the proportion of employees working in units of at least 500 employees fell from a half to a third between 1972 and 1987. Over the same period, the number working in units of under 100 employees grew in absolute as well as relative terms. These trends will surely continue, though not necessarily at the same rate, as small specialist manufacturing firms gain further ground. The shift from manufacturing to services, where workplaces are much smaller, accentuates the drop in workplace size across the economy as a whole.

In fact the division which is most significant electorally is between workplaces where under twenty-five people are employed and the rest. Among the working class Labour does a dozen or so points better among those who said that twenty-five or more people were employed at their place of work (Table A.7). Hence, the movement towards smaller workplaces is at least a minor factor counting against Labour.

Table A.7 Party by Size of Workplace, Within the Working Class, 1987

	Under 25 employees %	25 and over employees %
Conservative	34	29
Labour	41	53
Alliance	21	17

Note: Size of workplace is given by respondents and is not wholly accurate.
Source: BSA (1987).

Trade Union Membership

The massive drop in membership of trade unions in the 1980s is greater than can be accounted for by the rise in unemployment (Table A.8). Nowadays, barely one-half of members of the working class currently with jobs are in a union, compared to more like two-thirds in 1979. And less than one-third of routine non-manual workers are union members. Although the rate of decrease in membership has slowed since the early 1980s there is no prospect of a quick return to the record level of the late 1970s.

Table A.8 Trade Union Membership

	1975	1977	1979	1981	1983	1985	1986
Membership (millions)	12.0	12.8	13.3	12.1	11.2	10.7	10.5
Percentage of working population	47.2	50.1	51.1	46.6	41.6	38.4	37.1

Source: Social Trends; 1986 – Economic Trends (adjusted for compatability).

The social composition of union membership has also changed substantially. Forty per cent of members are women, compared to around a quarter in the mid-1970s. White collar unionists now make up nearly half of the membership. By 1987, about 30 per cent of members were in the salariat!

Union membership is certainly associated with Labour voting. For example, about 43 per cent of members voted Labour in

1987, substantially greater than the 32 per cent Labour achieved overall. However, it is not clear that union membership in itself greatly increases the likelihood of a person voting Labour. For union membership is usually and increasingly a matter of choice, especially among white collar workers. Membership could be associated with voting Labour because Labour supporters are more likely to join unions in the first place. It seems that union membership has some independent impact on voting, but only a very limited one. This means that the decline in union membership since 1979 cannot explain much of Labour's lost share of the vote.

The more important problem has been Labour's decline among manual union members. In this traditional heartland Labour's vote fell from 73 per cent in 1964 to 48 per cent in 1987. By contrast Labour's support held steady among the expanding category of white collar trade unionists (Crewe, 1989). Clearly many working-class trade unionists no longer link their union membership to their political allegiance.

State Dependency and Unemployment

During the 1980s there has been a huge growth in the number of people living on state pensions or unemployment/supplementary benefit. Between 1979 and 1986 the number of recipients of supplementary benefit grew from 3.0 to 4.9 million.

One might expect those dependent upon the state to be more inclined to vote Labour. Unfortunately, these people cannot generally be identified from survey data. However, within social groups, Labour does perform better among the unemployed compared to those in work. But the difference is only in single figures. This is a small advantage, in view of Labour's commitment to improve both the job prospects and the lot of those dependent upon the state. Thus this social change does not seem to have helped Labour much among those most affected by it. With unemployment falling and the size of the pensionable age group stable until the next century, trends in state dependency will not help Labour electorally in the short term.

Other Social Changes

Housing Tenure

The long-term trend towards greater home-ownership in Britain has accelerated in the 1980s. In preceding decades both owner-occupied and local authority tenancies had grown at the expense of the private rented sector. But as Table A.9 shows, under the Thatcher government expansion in home-ownership has resulted in the contraction of both other types of occupancy.

Table A.9 Housing Stock Tenure (percentages)

	1951 %	1961 %	1971 %	1976 %	1980 %	1982 %	1984 %	1986 %	1988 %
Owner occupied	30	43	50	54	55	59	61	63	65
Council dwellings	18	27	31	32	32	29	28	27	25
Private rented dwellings	52	30	19	15	13	12	11	10	10

Source: Social Trends; Regional Trends; Housing and Construction Statistics.

The pace of change has been much the same in every part of Great Britain. In each country or region the proportion of homes which were owner occupied increased in the narrow range of eight to eleven percentage points between 1976 and 1986. However, home-ownership remains considerably lower in Scotland. An eight point increase here still meant that only 42 per cent of homes were owner occupied, compared to 65 per cent in England and 68 per cent in Wales.

The future pace of change clearly depends somewhat on government policy. In the absence of new initiatives, home-ownership can be expected to reach a plateau before too long. None the less, by the next election two-thirds of the electorate, probably more, will be living in owner-occupied housing.

Housing is an important influence on voting, albeit one which reflects the electoral influence of neighbourhoods and income as well as the direct economic interests of home-ownership. As Table A.10 shows, Labour does about thirty points better among those living in council houses than among those in owner-occupied homes.

Table A.10 Party by Housing, 1987

	Owner occupied %	Council tenant %	Other rented %
Conservative	50	23	42
Labour	27	57	27
Alliance	22	18	29

Source: BSA (1987).

Though Labour has a bigger lead among council tenants than the Conservatives have among home-owners, this counts for a lot less. If Labour remains twenty-three points behind among home-owners, it would need an eighty point lead among council tenants to catch the Conservatives in popular support! But a smaller improvement for Labour among home-owners would have a much more dramatic effect. If Labour retains a thirty-four point lead among tenants, a reduction in the gap among owners to a little under ten points would bring the parties level. In practice the party needs more support in both groups – Labour achieved 70 per cent support among council tenants in 1964 – but should remember that the votes of many more home-owners are available.

Changes in housing tenure have obviously worked against Labour. A projection of the 1964 patterns of voting within housing groups on to the 1986 distribution in housing shows that Labour would have lost six to seven percentage points from changes in the size of housing groups, mostly to the Conservatives. However, changes in housing do not work wholly on top of class changes. Many new home-owners are also newly middle class, so there is a danger of double counting here. Having controlled for class changes, the expected extra impact of housing is not great. Yet we might also say that once changes in housing are controlled for, the expected impact of class changes is not as large as it at first appears! The point then is that the dual changes in class and housing were likely to help the Conservatives a good deal, but not doubly so. If patterns of voting within combined class and housing groups were the same in 1987 as in 1964, the Labour vote would be some ten percentage points lower.

Finally, evidence on whether council house sales has increased Conservative support among those who opted to buy is inconclusive (Crewe, 1989; Heath *et al.*, 1989). But as sales have so far affected only about 7 per cent of the electorate, any effect will have had little impact on the overall party balance. The housing issue concerns much broader associations. Labour needs to erode the perception that home-owners do best out of the Conservatives and that Labour is mainly concerned with council tenants. High mortgage rates, as seen in 1988–9, give the party the opportunity to show that its policies will be more beneficial to the home-owning majority.

Shares

When Mrs Thatcher came to power about 6 per cent of the population owned shares. This figure changed little in the next five years but took off in 1985. By early 1987, before British Airways was sold, the proportion of adults owning shares was in the range 18–20 per cent. Non-owners with share-owning spouses increase further the numbers with an interest in shares. Twenty-five per cent of the 1987 BSA sample said that they or their spouse owned shares (including unit trusts) quoted on the Stock Exchange. Future flotations of building societies may increase this figure substantially.

Not surprisingly, the Conservatives enjoy most support from shareholders – 53 per cent according to the 1987 BSA survey, with just 17 per cent identifying with Labour (representing 15 per cent of Labour supporters). But of course, shareholders are more middle class than the electorate as a whole. Controlling for class thus reduces the differences between shareholders and non-shareholders. For example, within the salariat Labour had the support of 12 per cent of shareholders and 24 per cent of non-holders. In the working class, about 15 per cent of whom owned shares in 1987, Labour's support runs between fifteen and twenty points lower among owners compared to non-owners. These are significant differences but are surely due mainly to the pre-existing allegiances of those who are able and choose to buy shares (Crewe, 1989; Heath *et al.*, 1989). The primary effect of the growth in share ownership has been to reinforce Conservative support rather than to extend it.

Gender

Historically, a slightly higher proportion of men than women have voted Labour (Table A.11). The Conservatives, in contrast, have done a bit better among women. But gender differences in turnout and party preferences have declined and were never very large anyway.

Table A.11 Percentage of Men and Women Voters Who Voted Labour, 1964–83

	1964	1966	1970	Feb 1974	Oct 1974	1979	1983	1987
Men	47	54	48	42	45	38	30	33
Women	47	51	42	40	40	38	28	31

Source: BES; Gallup (1987).

Nowadays, the Conservatives do no better among women than men. However, gender differences have not disappeared, since in many surveys Labour still gets a couple of per cent less from women than men. Among young women, though, the situation is reversed. In 1987, Labour's vote went up by eleven points among women aged 18–24 compared to an increase of just two points among young men. This did not just reflect a short-term impact of Labour's campaign emphasis on social issues. By the first quarter of 1989 Labour led by nineteen points among women aged 18–24 compared to level pegging among men of the same age.

Most women are not primarily concerned about 'women's issues'. However, more women than men are concerned about the essential public services and the risks of nuclear energy; fewer are concerned about defence and law and order and less prefer the Conservatives on these issues; and more women than men are pessimistic about the economy.

The danger of targeting women is that it will lead Labour away from the core issues of defence, law and order and the economy where Labour's real weaknesses lie. Labour needs more votes among men and women alike and this requires a general strategy rather than a narrow appeal. There is little point in targeting young women if Labour is doing well among them already. Nevertheless, these findings suggest that overall progress might lead to greater gains among women. Will 1991 be the first British general election in which Labour voting is higher among women than men?

The increased participation of women in the workforce has been a factor working against a Conservative lead among women. About 43 per cent of all those currently in paid work (employed or self-employed) are women. Table A.12 shows that though the trend will continue, it is expected to do so at a much slower rate.

Table A.12 Workforce by Gender, 1954–95

	1954 %	1975 %	1987 %	Projection 1995 %
Women	32	38	43	44
Men	68	62	57	56

Source: IER (1988).

Of course, the rise in female employment is associated with the ongoing increase in part-time working – from 14 per cent of all those in work in 1971 to 21 per cent in 1987.

Age

A major social change in Britain in the next thirty years will be the ageing of the population. This will not happen steadily, though. Indeed, there is likely to be no relative growth in the numbers of people of pensionable age in the 1990s. This will be followed by a fairly small increase in the first decade of the new century and a sharp rise thereafter. (However, the 85+ age group, a small proportion of the total population, will double in this century.) In the more immediate future the most significant change will be a fall in the number of young people, as Table A.13 shows.

These changes could work against Labour. For the age groups do vary in their voting behaviour, though the differences are quite small. In the 1987 election, Labour did about four

Table A.13 Age Structure, 1985–2021

| | 1985 % | Projections | | | | |
		1991 %	1996 %	2001 %	2011 %	2021 %
15–29	29.2	27.7	24.7	22.8	24.0	23.7
30–44	24.8	26.0	27.0	28.1	23.3	21.8
45–pensionable	23.6	23.5	25.4	26.4	28.7	28.3
Pensionable age	22.4	22.8	22.8	22.8	23.9	26.1

Source: OPCS, Population Projections: mid 1985-based (London: HMSO, 1986).

percentage points better among 18–29 year olds than among other age groups (Table A.14).

This is not a regular phenomenon. In the elections of 1974, 1979 and 1983 Labour did not do significantly better among the young. It is the relatively poor performance by the Conservatives among the young which has been more consistent. Since 1970, their share among those aged 18–29 has been at least 5 per cent less than among the 30+ age group. In addition, the Conservatives tend to do best among those aged at least 60.

Though the Conservatives are favoured by, first, the drop in the number of young people, and then the rise in the older population, the electoral effect will be small. If the voting patterns within each age group remain stable, even by 2021 the Conservative share of the vote would rise by only between 0.5 and 1 per cent, at the expense of both Labour and the centre. Even this may be an exaggeration of the electoral effect. For not all the difference in voting by age groups is a 'life-cycle' effect, whereby some people drift towards conservatism with age. One reason the Conservatives do better among the elderly is simply that their middle-class supporters live longer than working-class

Table A.14 Voting by Age Group, 1987

	18–29 %	30–44 %	45–64 %	65 and over %
Conservative	36	41	44	47
Labour	35	31	31	31
Alliance	26	26	22	19

Source: Harris/ITN Exit Poll.

people. With such factors discounted, the expected effect of the changes in age distribution is a drop in Labour's vote of only a small fraction of one percentage point.

Ethnic Minorities

Ethnic minorities made up 4.5 per cent of the population in 1986 (2.4 million people). The rate of increase is currently about 90,000 a year, but the minority population is eventually expected to stabilise at about 7 per cent of the total. The population will be over nine-tenths white for the foreseeable future. So non-white population growth is only a marginal benefit to Labour. Indeed, given low registration and turnout among Afro-Carib-beans, the proportion of voters who are non-white will remain lower than their share of the population.

However, what non-whites lack in numbers is partly made up for in location. Ethnic minorities are overrepresented in mar-ginal seats, notably in London (e.g. Battersea, Slough) and the Midlands (e.g. Nottingham East and South). In London, nearly a quarter of Labour's support comes from people of Asian or Afro-Caribbean origin. It is particularly important for Labour to mobilise its natural support in such seats. Registration cam-paigns might be crucial in some, for there is no doubt that Labour still does very well among ethnic minorities, especially among those living in areas where the minority population is concentrated. In national surveys, in 1988, Labour commanded at least fourteen points more support among those of Asian origin, and thirty-nine points more among Afro-Caribbeans, than among white voters.

Education

The main effect of education on party support (Table A.15) is among those with a degree, where Conservative support is lower than in all other qualification groups. The Alliance is strong among degree-holders and Labour, too, does well considering that most of these people belong to the salariat.

By combining data from the 1985 to 1987 BSA surveys to increase the sample size, we find that Conservative support among degree-holders in the salariat runs about 20 per cent below that among the rest of the class. On the basis of these

Table A.15 Party by Highest Educational Qualification, 1987

	Degree	Profes- sional	A-level	O-level	CSE	None
Percentage of sample	8	13	9	19	8	42
	%	%	%	%	%	%
Conservative	31	55	50	50	45	38
Labour	33	17	30	27	35	42
Alliance	33	28	20	21	18	18

Source: BSA (1987).

figures, if one-half of the salariat in Britain had degrees instead of just a quarter, this alone might cost the Conservatives 1.5 per cent of the total vote.

The proportion of the electorate who hold a degree will continue to rise for decades, as a natural consequence of generational turnover. Fifteen per cent of those aged 25–34 who were interviewed for the 1985–7 BSA surveys said that they had a degree, and the participation rate by young people in higher education is projected by the DES to rise to 19 per cent by the year 2000. These figures are well above the current proportion of 7–8 per cent of graduates in the population. If the Conservatives continue to do 20 per cent worse among degree-holders, they will lose about one and a half percentage points as the proportion of the whole electorate holding (or studying for) a degree increases to 15 per cent. However, assuming steady graduation rates, this could take half a century.

Parental Influences

Voting behaviour is influenced by the social and political environment in which people grow up, but this is a difficult factor to measure. However, figures for recalled parental class and party support suggest that such effects should have helped Labour in the 1980s. For more people grew up in working-class households than are currently in the working class; and more people report 'Labour parents' than Conservative ones.

Since much of the new middle class is drawn from the old working class this should limit the damage to Labour caused by the shift to middle-class jobs. Some Labour support is carried into the middle class. But this 'bridge' into the middle class will not remain open for ever. In the next century the middle class will become more self-recruiting, reflecting the occupational transformation taking place now. At some point in the next century, most voters will not only have white collar jobs but will also come from white collar backgrounds. So the task of expanding Labour's base in the middle class is likely to become harder. This remains a vital task, though, since to compete for power consistently in the longer term, Labour's underlying support in the middle class must be well above its current level.

Turning to the political environment during childhood, there has been a sharp rise in the number of people claiming that their father and/or mother voted for or preferred Labour (Table A.16).

Table A.16 Percentage of All Respondents Recalling Parental Support for the Labour and Conservative Parties

	1964	1966	1970	Feb 1974	1979	1983
Father – Labour	30	31	38	39	42	45
– Conservative	27	24	27	27	28	25
Mother – Labour	21	21	33		36	42
– Conservative	24	23	28		29	27

Note: For example, the 1983 figures show that 45 per cent of respondents recall a Labour father but only 25 per cent recall a Conservative father.
Source: BES.

Though the extent of Labour recall is surprising, the trend is expected. It reflects the decline in the proportion of the electorate brought up before the rise of the Labour Party in the early part of this century. But recall of Labour voting among parents cannot be expected to continue increasing. In 1983, for the first time, the proportion of young people recalling parental support for Labour was noticeably *less* than among the middle age groups. Our simulations suggest that at the turn of the century, the proportion of electors recalling Labour parents will be much the same as in 1983. But even this means that those believing that their parents voted Labour are likely to outnumber current Labour voters for a long time to come. This gives Labour some link, albeit a tenuous and historic one, with substantial numbers of current non-Labour voters, including middle-class ones.

Of course, how valuable this is to Labour is questionable. In 1983, only 45 per cent of voters who recalled that their parents supported Labour said that they voted Labour. However, this is much greater than the 9 per cent of those with Conservative parents who voted Labour and within each social class Labour did best among those with Labour parents. So though parental socialisation clearly did not prevent Labour's decline, it may have prevented an even worse collapse. Indeed, the influence of parental factors may well have been sufficient in 1983 to stop Labour sliding those further couple of per cent into third place.

Region and Neighbourhood

As is well known, the Labour and Conservative shares of the vote vary a good deal between different parts of the country (Table A.17).

Table A.17   1987 Election Results

	England			Scotland	Wales
	South %	*Midlands* %	*North* %	%	%
Conservative	51.8	47.8	36.6	24.0	29.5
Labour	20.9	30.0	42.1	42.4	45.1
Alliance	26.8	21.8	21.0	19.2	17.9
Nationalist				14.0	7.3

Source: Butler and Kavanagh, 1988.

These regional variations cannot be accounted for solely by differences in social structure. They reflect two further impacts on voting. The first is the 'neighbourhood effect' of the local social and political environment. For example, middle-class voters in mainly working-class, pro-Labour areas are more likely to vote Labour than their counterparts in largely middle-class, pro-Conservative areas. The contraction of both the working class and areas of Labour strength means that Labour now gains less, and loses more, from this 'multiplier effect' than in the past.

The second factor is growing regional economic disparities. These are evident in economic perceptions, both of the national economy and household circumstances. The regional differences in perceptions are not large enough to explain more than a little of the regional variations in voting. But, together, the neighbourhood effect and economic disparities are likely to sustain, and perhaps accentuate, the North–South electoral divide.

Combining Social Characteristics: A More Detailed Picture of the British Electorate

By combining the data from four BSA surveys, 1984–7, we can produce a more detailed picture of how social characteristics influence party support both singly and in combination. Our classification is based on the three characteristics which have the strongest association with voting in the late 1980s – class, housing and region. In addition, notable production sector divisions within the salariat and the working class are built in. Even with 9,000 cases, not all the possible categories could sensibly be retained. So very small groups were added to others. The resulting twenty-six category classification is listed in Table A.18. The size of each group as a percentage of the total is given, as well as the percentages of party identification within it. The figures for the smaller groups are subject to substantial sampling error of party support. In all groups, Labour's likely electoral support is overestimated by party identification, particularly when, as in this case, three of the surveys were conducted in mid-term. None the less, Labour's relative position in the groups is probably estimated reliably.

Table A.18 highlights several of the points made earlier in this appendix. Labour is strongest in categories which are shrinking – the working class, council tenants, those in the North/West and those working in nationalised industries. Most striking are the differences *within* the working class. The expanding 'new' working class of home-owners in the South/East is at least as inclined to identify with the Conservatives as with Labour. It is worth comparing this, the largest single group in our classification, with one of working-class council tenants from the North/West (group 21) (Table A.19).

Table A.18 Social Groups in Britain: Combinations of Class, Housing, Region, and Sector 1984–7

Group	Class	Housing	Region	Sector	Size	Party identification (Row percentages)				
						C	L	A	NP	RL
1	Salariat	Own	N/W	Priv	4.2	52	17	22	10	24
2	"	Own	N/W	Public	3.7	34	29	26	11	16
3	"	Own	S/E	Priv	8.7	63	12	17	8	26
4	"	Own	S/E	Public	4.5	43	22	28	8	21 =
5	"	LA	Both	"	1.9	33	33	18	17	12
6	"	P.rent	Both	"	1.9	42	22	23	14	21 =
7	Routine	Own	N/W	"	4.8	32	32	21	15	13 =
8	Non-manual	Own	S/E	"	7.5	50	18	22	11	23
9	"	LA	N/W	"	1.4	16	49	17	18	5 =
10	"	LA	S/E	"	1.7	27	31	24	18	15
11	"	P.rent	Both	"	1.4	41	27	18	14	18 =
12	Petty-	All	N/W	"	3.4	44	27	11	18	18 =
13	bourgeoisie	All	S/E	"	4.9	60	15	13	13	25
14	Manual	Own	N/W	"	2.0	37	40	16	8	11
15	foremen	Own	S/E	"	2.3	42	23	21	14	20
16	"	LA & P.rent	Both	"	2.5	22	49	11	17	5 =
17	Working	Own & P.rent	N/W	Not N	7.9	21	48	17	15	8
18	class	Own & P.rent	N/W	Natls	1.2	14	67	10	9	2
19	"	Own & P.rent	S/E	Not N	11.0	34	32	17	17	13 =
20	"	Own & P.rent	S/E	Natls	1.5	25	46	14	15	9
21	"	LA	N/W	Not N	6.2	11	64	8	17	3
22	"	LA	N/W	Natls	1.1	6	79	7	7	1
23	"	LA	S/E	"	7.0	18	49	14	20	5 =

			Size	C	L	A	NP	RL
24	No class assigned	Own	Both	3.5	38	28	15	20	17
25	"	LA	Both	2.7	11	59	9	21	4
26	"	P.rent	Both	1.1	25	42	19	15	10
	TOTALS			100.0	35	34	17	14	

Source: BSA (1984-7).

Key for Table A.18

Size — Percentage of the whole sample (the table is based on 9,246 respondents, so each per cent equals about ninety cases and no category numbers less than 100)

C — Conservative party identification

L — Labour party identification

A — Liberal, Social Democrat or Alliance identification

NP — No party identification (none or don't know) plus a small number identifying with other than a major party

RL — Rank order of Labour identification – highest to lowest

Class — Goldthorpe scheme, with residual 'no class' category for cases when lack of data prevented classification

Housing — Own – lives in owner-occupied housing
LA – Local authority (council) housing
P.rent – Private sector rented housing

Region — N/W – North/West Britain
S/E – South/East Britain

Sector — Priv – private sector
Not N – Not nationalised industry
i.e. all private sector and rest of public sector
Natls – nationalised industry

Table A.19 Characteristics of Two Working-class Groups

Group 19 Working-class, owner-occupied or private rented housing, in the South/East, not working in a nationalised industry.

Group 21 Working-class, local authority housing, in the North/West, not working in a nationalised industry.

	Group 19 %	Group 21 %	All respondents %
Increase taxes and spend more on services	40	49	46
More state ownership of industry	13	22	14
Britain should rid itself of nuclear weapons	25	33	26
Labour Party is extreme	38	28	44
Conservative Party is extreme	42	57	49
Would place self in low income group (subjective viewpoint)	53	78	47
Household income fallen behind prices in last year	47	68	48
In median to top income group (based on reported income)	60	24	60
Car owners	77	34	71
Trade union members	27	23	27
Self-rated social class: middle	17	9	27

Source: BSA (1984–7).

We find great differences between the groups on economic perceptions and, especially, more objective measures of economic circumstances (household income and car ownership). Many more in the 'new' working class are, economically, optimistic and affluent. Overall, figures for the 'new' working class are very close to those for the total sample. We showed earlier that the target voters for Labour are a representative section of the whole electorate. We now find that even if Labour chooses to concentrate on the new working class, it will be addressing a group which is also representative on a range of measures.

Finally, note that Labour leads among working-class home-owners in the North/West. Labour's identification among this group (number 17) is sixteen points higher than among the equivalent group in the South/East (number 19). Yet on the measures of political attitudes and economic circumstances there is only a small average difference between the two groups. So this indicates that greater affluence for sections of the working class does not consign Labour to second place among them. Social change continues to make it more difficult for Labour, but political action can still raise Labour's standing in virtually all groups.

References

Abrams, M. (1964) 'Opinion Polls and Party Propaganda', *Public Opinion Quarterly*, vol. 28, pp. 13–20.

After we finished this book, we discovered that Mark Abrams had said most of it in seven pages twenty-five years ago. So much for the changing voter!

Abrams, M. and Rose, R. (1960) *Must Labour Lose?* (Harmondsworth, Middlesex: Penguin).

Rita Hinden's commentary concluded 'Yes, it must' because of crumbling class solidarity, the declining appeal of public ownership and divisions within the party. But Richard Rose's caution proved more accurate and is still relevant: 'We can understand voters much better if we give up the illusion that there exists somewhere a magic formula for infallibly predicting what the electorate will decide at the next election.'

Berrington, H. (1989) 'British Public Opinion and Nuclear Weapons', in C. Frazer and C. Marsh (eds) *Public Opinion and Nuclear Weapons* (London: Macmillan).

Butler, D. (1986) *Governing Without a Majority* (Basingstoke, Hants: Macmillan).

A readable handbook on what to do when the hung Parliament comes.

Butler, D. and Kavanagh, D. (1988) *The British General Election of 1987* (Basingstoke, Hants: Macmillan).

Thirteenth in the series. Includes a definitive analysis of the constituency results by John Curtice and Michael Steed.

Central Statistical Office (1989) *Social Trends 19* (London: HMSO).

A wealth of statistical information about British society.

Crewe, I. (1988) 'Has the Electorate become Thatcherite?' in R. Skidelsky (ed.), *Thatcherism* (London: Chatto & Windus) pp. 25–50.

No, says Crewe, arguing soundly that cohesion, purpose and success take precedence over policy and ideology in voters' eyes.

Crewe, I. (1989) 'The decline of labour and the decline of Labour: social and electoral trends in post-war Britain', paper for the Conference on Popular Power in Post-industrial Societies, City University of New York.

Shows that the Labour Party has declined further and faster than its social base. Considers four strategies Labour could adopt for the future but seems doubtful that any of them would work.

Crewe, I. and Fox, A. (1984) *British Parliamentary Constituencies* (London: Faber and Faber).

A useful compendium; more census statistics than Waller but now out of print.

Crosland, A. (1960) *Can Labour Win?* (London: Fabian Society).

Predicted a 2 per cent decline in Labour's vote at each election unless 'Labour can present itself as a progressive, national social-democratic party'. That would have given Labour 28 per cent in 1987, which Labour achieved one election early.

Heath, A., Jowell, R. and Curtice, J. (1985) *How Britain Votes* (Oxford: Pergamon).

The latest (and most readable) in a series of academic election surveys which provide much material for this book. Referred to as BES (British Election Study) in the text.

Heath, A., Jowell, R. and Curtice, J. (1988) 'Partisan Dealignment Revisited', paper presented at the Political Studies Association Annual Conference.

Suggests there has been no clear increase in electoral volatility over the last twenty-five years. The apparent increase simply reflects people turning away from Labour. This usefully corrects exaggerated claims of a wide-open electorate.

Heath, A., Jowell, R. and Curtice, J. (1989) *The Extension of Popular Capitalism* (Strathclyde University, Department of Politics: Papers on Government and Politics, No. 60).

Concludes that council house buyers and first-time share owners did not become more disposed to the Conservatives than they were already. However, Crewe (1989) suggests council house buyers do become more Conservative. All agree those council tenants who remain are concentrated increasingly on the bottom of the social scale.

Heath, A. and McDonald, S. K. (1987) 'Social Change and the Future of the Left', *The Political Quarterly*, vol. 88, pp. 364–77.

Suggests that social change does not rule out a Labour victory and argues that in the short run parties gain or lose support across the board. Advocates extending union membership as a way of expanding Labour's base.

Institute for Employment Research (1988) *Review of the Economy and Employment: Occupational Assessment* (University of Warwick, Coventry CV4 7AL).

The source for many of the employment projections in the appendix. Referred to as IER in the text.

Jowell, R., *et al.* (eds) *British Social Attitudes* (Gower Publishing, Gower House, Croft Road, Aldershot, Hants, GU11 3HR).

Annual surveys of British public opinion conducted by Social and Community Planning Research. Widely used in this book. Referred to as BSA in the text.

Leadbeater, C. (1987) *The Politics of Prosperity* (Fabian Tract 523, The Fabian Society, 11 Dartmouth Street, London SW1H 9BN).

Argues that economic competitiveness and social citizenship must reinforce each other as the basis of Labour's programme.

Lipsey, D., Shaw, A. and Willman, J. (1989) *Labour's Electoral Challenge* (London: Fabian Research Series 352).

Shows that public opinion has, if anything, moved to the left under Thatcher but that social trends have worked against Labour. Concludes that Labour must rebuild general credibility, as well as reformulate specific policies, if it is to have a serious chance of office.

Mackie, T. and Rose, R. (1982) *The International Almanac of Electoral History* (London: Macmillan).

Definitive lists of election results in Western nations. Annual updates appear in the *European Journal of Political Research*.

Miller, W., Brand, J. and Jordan, M. (1982) 'On the Power or Vulnerability of the British Press', *British Journal of Political Science*, vol. 12, pp. 357–73.

Suggests that although any one newspaper has little power to mould readers' attitudes, the impact of an overall media consensus can be considerable.

MORI, *British Public Opinion* (32 Old Queen St, London SW1H 9HP).

Covers a wide range of polling topics and includes a digest of all major published polls. Published ten times a year.

Page, I., Shapiro, R. and Dempsey, G. (1987) 'What Moves Public Opinion?', *American Political Science Review*, vol. 81, pp. 23–43.

The answer, in order, is TV news commentators, experts, research reports, and popular Presidents. Interest groups and unpopular Presidents lack credibility and, therefore, impact.

Rentoul, J. (1989) *Me and Mine: The Triumph of the New Individualism* (London: Unwin Hyman).

Using polls and qualitative research, Rentoul argues that Mrs Thatcher has failed to shift the electorate away from collective values. Her success is based on a divided opposition and economic growth.

Social Surveys (Gallup Poll) Ltd, *Gallup Political Index* (202 Finchley Road, London NW3 6BL).

Gallup's monthly reports are an invaluable source on changes in British public opinion. Widely quoted in this book.

Waller, R. (1987) *The Almanac of British Politics* (Beckenham, Kent: Croom Helm).

This seat-by-seat analysis of every constituency is a fine achievement.

FABIAN SERIES

IMPRISONED BY OUR PRISONS
by Vivien Stern

Overcrowded, mismanaged, hidden from view and ignored – who do our prisons serve, and what are they for? Do they protect society from a dangerous criminal threat? Punish those who have gone astray? Re-educate those who have – for whatever reason – fallen foul of the law? Or are they an outmoded, ineffectual and unimaginative response to a variety of social problems?

Vivien Stern unlocks the prison doors and suggests new, more humane approaches to the problems 'inside'. She examines the concerns of the men and women who live and work within them, exposing the abuses of power, the denial or rights, and the humiliation and degradation that the system imposes.

Arguing against prevalent calls for stiffer sentences, she explores the possibilities for reducing the use of custodial penalties and easing the tensions within our overpopulated prison buildings. She also demonstrates a variety of solutions from abroad that might easily be implemented here. Some would transform our prisons into infinitely more humane institutions; others are shown to have decidedly sinister implications.

This challenging and far-sighted book will cause us to re-evaluate our responsibility for our prisons, and for those we confine in them.

Vivien Stern is Director for the National Association for the Care and Resettlement of Offenders.

ISBN 004 4452977

FABIAN SERIES

GOODBYE COUNCIL HOUSING
by David Clapham

The public housing sector, under attack from the Government and plagued by its own shortcomings, is in a crisis which could lead to its demise. But – since 1919 – council housing has been seen as a key instrument for achieving social objectives in housing, and this crisis therefore raises crucial questions. Is council housing an effective way of achieving these objectives? What strategy should the Government's opponents pursue?

This provocative contribution to the debate over the future of council housing will stimulate discussion about social objectives in housing, and about alternatives to council housing which aim to give tenants more control over their housing situation.

David Clapham is Assistant Director of the Centre for Housing Research at the University of Glasgow. He has written extensively on council housing and housing co-operatives.

ISBN 004 4452969

FABIAN SERIES

COMPETITIVE SOCIALISM
Austin Mitchell

One of Labour's central problems is how to develop an economic policy which is both socialist and in tune with the new expectations of the electorate. Austin Mitchell argues that the two are entirely compatible, and that British society and socialism can be transformed by a policy of economic expansion.

Austin Mitchell is MP for Great Grimsby and an economist.

April 0 04 440431 X

FABIAN SERIES

REFORMING WHITEHALL
Clive Ponting

A 19th century institution in the late 20th century: closed, unaccountable and inadequate. That is how Clive Ponting sees Whitehall, and few people are better qualified than he to make such comments. In *Reforming Whitehall* he describes what must happen if the system is to lose this widely held reputation and become the efficient and open machine we need.

Clive Ponting is a writer and former civil servant.

April 004 4404336